Educational Accountability

Educational Accountability

Professional Voices from the Field

Edited by

Kenneth D. Gariepy
University of Alberta, Canada

Brenda L. Spencer
University of Alberta, Canada

Jean-Claude Couture
The Alberta Teachers' Association, Canada

SENSE PUBLISHERS
ROTTERDAM/BOSTON/TAIPEI

Cataloguing-in-Publication Data

Educational accountability : professional voices from the field / edited by Kenneth D. Gariepy,
    Brenda L. Spencer and Jean-Claude (J-C) Couture.
    p. cm
    Includes bibliographical references and index.
    ISBN 978-90-8790-900-0 (pbk.)

1. Educational accountability. 2. Educational accountability – Alberta. 3. Educational
evaluation – Alberta. 4. Education and state – Alberta. I. Gariepy, Kenneth D. (Kenneth
Donald), 1970- II. Spencer, Brenda L. III. Couture, Jean-Claude, 1955-

LB2806.22
379.15--dc22

ISBN: 978-90-8790-900-0 (paperback)
ISBN: 978-90-8790-901-7 (hardback)
ISBN: 978-90-8790-902-4 (e-book)

Published by: Sense Publishers,
P.O. Box 21858, 3001 AW
Rotterdam, The Netherlands
http://www.sensepublishers.com

Printed on acid-free paper

Not everything that counts can be counted, and not everything that can be counted counts.

–Albert Einstein

TABLE OF CONTENTS

TABLE OF CONTENTS

DISCLAIMER

The views and opinions expressed in these chapters are those of the authors and do not necessarily reflect those of their employers.

FOREWORD

We live in an age of accountability, of outcomes and indicators, of measures and scores, as well as in an age with a surfeit of media eagerly waiting to report "the findings" that are generated. This is the result of the scientific revolution, which promoted systems and mathematical thinking about the natural world and later about business processes in the economic world. Thinking in this way, in turn, generated rich information that has made both our understanding of the natural world and the productivity of our businesses much greater than they were in the past. Thus, it should come as no surprise that successful ways of thinking in these areas would be seen as the key to success in the human services area. But it is possible that this logical attempt to move ways of thinking from science and business to areas of human services may actually prove to be harmful, perhaps even impossible.

What is needed, of course, is brisk argument to help us understand the possibilities of and barriers to moving ideas across cultures, domains and fields of endeavour. That is what makes this book so timely and important. It questions the accountability systems being applied in Alberta, Canada, and by doing so, raises issues important to the entire world. It would be good if this book could start the dialogue needed to design sensible accountability systems.

There is nothing inherently Canadian about wanting to improve education; it is a goal of all democratic nations. And there is nothing Canadian about trying to build accountability schemes for monitoring the productivity and efficiency of a nation's educational system. Most of the costs of education, in most nations, are paid for by the public, and so most nations want and deserve some account of how their money is spent. What does seem uniquely Canadian to this American is the articulate opposition and passion of those who see the faults of many modern systems of school accountability. This is a book prodding us to think about the nature of education, its purposes and processes, and the effects contemporary systems of accountability have on curriculum, instruction and the lives of our students and teachers. The chapter authors have made me think more deeply about issues with which I thought I was already conversant.

One crucial issue raised in this book, in more than one place, is perhaps the oldest and most important one in education: What should be taught to our students? That is, what knowledge is of most worth? In the days when Canada and the USA had many people making a living from agriculture, hunting, mining and forestry, most people got by on low levels of literacy. When children followed their parents into the tailoring or the grocery business, the schools had a simple task, since the future was not hard to divine. But now all of us, youth in particular, face a VUCA world: a future that is Volatile, Uncertain, Complex, and Ambiguous. It's the nature of postmodern life and globalization. What knowledge is of most worth in such a world? After a full measure of literacy, numeracy and scientific knowledge is taught in our schools, what else is needed to succeed in a VUCA world?

Does a province or a state, through the design of its own assessments, have an answer to that question? They had better! Because we know that if the assessments are consequential, as they are in Alberta and throughout the U.S., then those assessments determine the curriculum enacted in our schools. Teachers and schools teach what is on tests that are consequential, and this often turns out to be the kind of knowledge that is divorced from precisely those skills that might be useful to individuals and governments in the near future. The chapters in this book make plain that the kinds of skills that might be useful in a VUCA world are not tapped by the assessments used, despite wonderful rhetoric to the contrary. Cheap and quick testing systems, common across North America, simply do not allow for the measurement of problem identification skills or skill in genuine problem solving; they fail to adequately measure creativity and critical media literacy; and they do not measure student skills in collaborative work. These tests rarely assess moral thinking and the skills needed for citizenship, yet every teacher in every school in North America will attest that those domains are a central part of their teaching mission.

These authors all want to see deep and broad learning in their schools, as do the provincial designers of the accountability system. But this book makes clear from the experience of other states and nations that this will not happen when high-stakes testing is the basis of an accountability system. The curriculum is always narrowed when teachers and schools are assessed by means of high-stakes testing. Depth of learning in the tested areas is sacrificed for breadth of coverage and whole topics and areas of the curriculum not covered on the tests are jettisoned form the curriculum so test scores will go up.

These authors also want to see an educational system that treats teachers as professionals, whose thoughts about curriculum and instruction are heard and respected. But experience in the U.S., England and many Asian countries, in particular, demonstrates that when high stakes assessments are used together with narrow assessment systems, teachers become pawns in a system of education that serves people and purposes they may not want to serve. The authors remind us that accountability systems are frequently based on a complete lack of trust in teachers. Teachers' judgments about children and ideas about curriculum are generally ignored in high-stakes testing environments Teachers are not treated in a democratic fashion, as a community of professionals whose opinions matter. This state of affairs was remarked upon by John Dewey, many years ago. His comment is relevant to what these authors are about. Dewey (1903) said:

> Until the public school system is organized in such a way that every teacher has some regular and representative way in which he or she can register judgment upon matters of educational importance, with the assurance that this judgment will somehow affect the school system, the assertion that the present system is not ... democratic seems to be justified .... What does democracy mean, save that the individual is to have a share in determining the conditions and the aims of his own work...? (pp. 195–197)

Dewey and the authors of this book remind us that the design of assessment systems needs to be about furthering democracy, as well as about improving performance, that it needs to be about the fullness of children's lives, as well as about the scores that they yield, and that it should be about depth of learning, and learning across a broad spectrum of human endeavours, not just about the kind of learning that prepares a student for a test. Readers will find chapters in this book to enrich a dialogue about assessment, for that is what is needed across the western world. In many provinces, states and nations there has been a loss of trust between professional educators and those in industry and government. This needs to be acknowledged and repaired, and that process begins with conversations about issues addressed in this book.

David C. Berliner
Phoenix, AZ
January, 2009

REFERENCE

Dewey, J. (1903). Democracy and education. *Elementary School Teacher*, 4(4), 193–204. doi: 10.1086/453309

PREFACE

IN PRAISE OF ACCOUNTABILITY

Critical of the ways that accountability is applied and enforced in public sector schools and classrooms, the writers in this book, along with other educators, might strike some readers as being against accountability in general and in all its manifestations. Is the book arguing that teachers, principals and professors should just be given the money and left alone to get on with the job? Far from it. The accountability agenda is much more complex than that.

Shouldn't all of us be accountable and be called to account from time to time in our lives and in our practices? Members of most religions believe that they will be called to account in an afterlife and this affects how they choose to live their lives here on Earth. The problem, of course, is that not all people are always right or good–not even teachers–and accountability belongs in their world as much as it does in any other.

The answer to excessive or ineffective accountability, therefore, can and should never be no accountability–a world in which there is only unrestricted and unregulated professional autonomy. When bridges and tunnels collapse because of insufficient diligence in engineering design, when patients die of hospital infections because physicians fail to fill out procedural checklists or even wash their hands, and when teachers are sarcastic to their students or slip out early from professional development sessions, the public is right to call professionals to account. The purpose of accountability, however, is not only to confront malpractice or even to prevent harm in the first place. It is also to improve performance by examining its impact, measuring quality and results and spurring people on to achieve even higher standards and greater improvement in the future. These things become possible when people, with others, have access to and are pressed to act on relevant information and data about their effectiveness.

I have seen much of this in a large-scale study I am conducting with Professor Alma Harris about organizations that perform beyond expectations in education, health, business and sports. Part of the study involves a local authority (school district) in a London borough with a predominantly Bangladeshi population. The authority was the worst performing in Britain in 1997 but now performs at or above the national average. In standardized achievement tests, examination results and rates of students going on to university, it now ranks as the most improved local authority in Britain. It has also significantly reduced achievement gaps in relation to children with special educational needs, those from cultural minorities and those on free school meals. The instigation of this dramatic turnaround occurred as a result of the visionary leadership of a new director (superintendent) who believed that "poverty is not an excuse for failure," that aspirations should be extremely high and that the effort to meet these aspirations should be pursued relentlessly, with a sense of great urgency. The data discussed above kept people focused and maintained and also inspired the sense of urgency. So far, the evidence seems to point to the advocates of accountability being right: that in industry, sports and public sector organizations alike, accountability, at its best, stimulates improvement, increases quality and promotes openness and transparency. No more will the professions be, as George Bernard Shaw once put it, "conspiracies against the laity."

QUESTIONING ACCOUNTABILITY

The educationally high-achieving Nordic countries have no word of their own for accountability. In an evaluation for the OECD of Finland's top-performing educational system and its approaches to leadership, my colleagues and I found that much of its effectiveness was explained by highly qualified teachers committed to a common educational and social mission, working together in cultures of what they called trust, cooperation and responsibility. Teachers directed this commitment towards all students their actions could potentially affect, not just towards those in their own classes or even in their own schools (Hargreaves, Halász & Pont, 2007).

If by accountability we mean responsibility, then we should call it exactly that; however, accountability usually means more. It often means, for example, answering to an external public or higher authority in order to prevent or deal with slacking off or wrongdoing. In this sense, accountability becomes a device to prevent people we do not trust from doing bad things, rather than a device that enables people we do trust to do good things. Accountability is sometimes a synonym for responsibility, but more often it is a substitute for it. Accountability is the remainder that is left when responsibility has been subtracted. It is a valuable and necessary remainder, but a remainder all the same.

A second meaning of accountability is transparency or openness. Consider the professions, for example, which, by nature, have tried to retain their status by securing a monopoly over exclusive and esoteric knowledge, sometimes by hiding it from or making it mysterious to the general public. This often occurs; try reading your medical diagnosis or a standards rubric produced by your child's school, for example.

So the call for more transparency is a good thing, and making test scores, examination results and even school inspection reports available to the public is often advocated in the interest of transparency. I have seen transparency go further than this, however, in an evaluation of a network of schools in England that showed how two thirds of the schools improved at twice the rate of the national average. This occurred partly because the schools' performance results were made transparent to each other and partly because the schools were willing to seek help from each other regarding the commitment and urgency I mentioned above. In this way, individual schools were transparent to their peers in the network.

Problems can arise, however, when rich processes of transparency such as this are replaced or reduced to the shallow transparency of reporting test results in fragmented systems of competitive market choice. They can also arise when transparency runs in only in one direction, as when governments and corporations are not prepared to be transparent as well. In this sense, it is interesting that economically and educationally high performing Finland also ranks high on international scores of corporate transparency. Reciprocal transparency is integral to democracy. One-way transparency is just top-down surveillance.

A third interpretation of accountability is simple "countability," as it is referred to in competitive performance rankings. The systems of comparative, numerical performance scores that include standardized test results are meant to inform choice, increase inter-school competition, lift educational standards and promote eventual economic competitiveness.

Remember, though, that in best business practice, the things that are counted as quality indicators authentically represent what the company and its staff are trying to achieve through common agreement. In public schools influenced by business-style metrics of quality, standards and targets, however, there is no such agreement about, nor confidence in, the validity of the metrics. The system then focuses more on "countability"–what can be easily measured– at the expense of other vital goals and purposes, for which no appropriate metrics have been developed at all.

Understand also that in the best businesses and national sports organizations that my colleagues and I are researching, the unit of win-lose competition is other similar businesses, national sporting teams or market sectors; it is not the different units, departments or brands within the organizations, with the exception of motivational instances of friendly, win-win rivalry.

In this vein, following best business practice, the appropriate unit of educational competition is not the neighbouring teacher or nearby school; it is other nations and education systems. When departments compete with departments in a company or schools compete for clients in a community, overall value is not increased. It is merely redistributed, with one unit rising at the expense of another and without common gains accruing overall.

Finally, when businesses test their products for quality control, they typically do not test every item but select a sample that is statistically large enough to generalize to the entire product population. Testing everything is, in business terms, inefficient, imprudent and a fatal cost to competitiveness and profitability. But the business-driven philosophy applied to public education is to test everyone by census rather than by sample. This is equally unnecessary statistically and profoundly wasteful financially. Over-testing in education is as profligate and imprudent as it is in business.

The chapters in this important and timely book offer thoughtful critiques of educational accountability from a multiplicity of professional perspectives, exposing, time after time, how the sincere pursuit of the loftier goals of public education is often overshadowed by performances that are easily counted. Together, they suggest that is neither time to retreat to the individual autonomy, professional self-interest and protectionism of the 1960s and 1970s nor to adopt the models and myths of corporate accountability that do not themselves reflect the actual practices of the very best businesses.

Let's put responsibility and transparency first and use accountability as a backup to check, in sampling terms, whether we truly achieve the quality we claim. Let's not attack or abandon criteria or indicators, but develop better and broader ones that reflect the rightful goals of public education and that help secure agreement among the highly qualified professionals who work so diligently towards them. Let's learn to let go a little politically in order to lift everyone's game professionally. There can be few better places to start than by reading this critical yet highly constructive book.

Andy Hargreaves
Thomas More Brennan Chair in Education
Boston College
February, 2009

REFERENCE

Hargreaves, A., Halász, G., & Pont, B. (2007). *School leadership for systemic improvement in Finland: A case study report for the OECD activity improving school leadership.* Retrieved February 18, 2009, from http://www.oecd.org/dataoecd/43/17/39928629.pdf

ACKNOWLEDGEMENTS

This book would not have been possible without the contributions and support of many individuals.

The authors, most of whom are full-time teachers and school leaders, carved out time from their busy schedules to work with us in preparing their manuscripts. Their enthusiasm and commitment to the book was greatly appreciated, and we learned immensely from our experiences with them during this collaborative project.

We would also like to thank all of the students of the University of Alberta's Spring 2008 graduate course, *Leadership in Educational Accountability: Sustaining Professional Learning and Innovation* and the many participants of the Alberta Teachers' Association's Spring 2008 Symposium for the contributions, discussions and debates that were so instrumental in the generation of ideas that are developed in this book's chapters. We are especially appreciative of the opportunities the authors had to interact with Drs. Andy Hargreaves, Stephen Murgatroyd and Pasi Sahlberg during the course of the Symposium weekend and the project.

In so many ways, the Alberta Teachers' Association and the Department of Educational Policies Studies at the University of Alberta were supportive of both the contributors' work and our efforts in moving the book forward. We are particularly grateful to our colleagues who acknowledge the importance of publishing a compilation representing professionals in the "field," whose perspectives and insights reflect the real work of educational accountability.

We also want to acknowledge the enormous contribution that our Co-Editor, Kenneth Gariepy, made to this project. His superb organizational and communication skills, his amazing technology, reference and information expertise, his care and understanding in working with individual authors and in keeping us all on track, his writing and editing prowess, his guidance through the publishing process, his many thoughtful words along the way and his sense of humour – not to mention the hours and hours of time spent – were way over and above what we expected. We would not have been able to see this project through had it not been for his unrelenting patience and commitment.

Brenda L. Spencer and J-C Couture

BRENDA L. SPENCER AND J-C COUTURE

INTRODUCTION

Transcending ideological and political boundaries, demands for public sector accountability have increased significantly over the past 25 years. At local, national, and international levels, accountability has become a key principle for policy development in Western, industrialized nations. As is the case in other public sectors, the pursuit of accountability in education has intensified. For more than two decades now, public education reforms have been based on the premise that accountability will improve efficiency and effectiveness and, to a great extent, changes occurring in today's educational institutions are changes initiated and driven by accountability policies.

Facilitating a range of localized responses to the increasing pressures of competing in the global economy and the legacy of the supposedly failed progressive public education systems of the 1960s and 1970s, new modes of accountability have become the means of restoring public trust. This is to be accomplished through a range of policies for:
- decentralized control of education to the school level for the purpose of promoting autonomy, responsiveness to local needs, choice and "market accountability" through competition
- increased central control over measures for monitoring effectiveness and ensuring "quality" education, such as programs for common curricula focusing on core subject areas and established levels and objectives for measuring competency
- standardized achievement and large-scale testing programs and, in some cases, the publication of the results of these high-stakes assessments
- heightened focus on standards for the training, qualification, supervision and evaluation of educators

This is the case in our own province, Alberta, where the current approach to educational accountability was introduced 15 years ago, during a time of restructuring, downsizing and funding cutbacks and where programs are now being reviewed for present or continuing effectiveness and future viability. In Alberta's education system, accountability policies have introduced another dimension of complexity to circumstances that have always been inherently challenging and are that are now increasingly complicated by the pressures of globalization. In the current context of an impending economic crisis which, in Alberta, follows hard on the heels of a period of unprecedented growth, educators at all levels and in all sites work to meet the needs of a diversity of students, to constantly adjust curriculum, teaching and learning objectives and pedagogical strategies and to fulfill the demands of decentralized administrative roles, all while facing the challenges related to the ever-increasing expectations of implementing, evaluating and sustaining myriad accountability policies. These demands are the concern of educators, researchers, and Alberta's Education Partners.[i]

Alberta's current school jurisdiction performance annual reporting processes are determined by the government's *accountability pillar*. According to the Ministry of Education, the *pillar* information

> demonstrates how well each district is doing in realizing expected outcomes and which areas require additional work. It also allows school boards to assess their achievement compared to provincial standards and to see how they have improved compared to their previous performance. (Alberta Education, 2009b)

The quantitative data gathered for and reported in the *pillar* results is what we would call an "empirical narrative"– a story about human intentions and consequences told with numbers. District *pillar* "report cards" attempt to illustrate a relationship between district data collected each year (i.e., annual survey results, student performance on government examinations, high school drop-out and completion rates) and the degree of relative success achieved in terms of meeting the learning needs of students. Yet, like all story-telling, these narratives, commonly referred to as "score cards," include and exclude particular ways of seeing life in Alberta schools. Never mind that, as the pre-eminent educational scholar, Linda McNeil (1986), has pointed out, "measurable outcomes may be the least significant results of learning" (p. 18).

According to education experts, the province of Alberta has the dubious distinction as one of the most robust examples of a command- and-control approach to educational accountability in Canada (Lessard & Brassard, 2005). Further, one of the overriding limitations of the government's current approach to accountability is that it is largely a story told to the public without much context. Report cards are published annually to provide an account of measures of achievement according to numerical value ranges that are colour-coded: red (very low), orange (low), yellow (intermediate), green (high), blue (very high). Invoking the all-too-familiar green/yellow/red metaphor is an attempt to signal meaning and significance. Yet these score cards confuse data with information, information with knowledge and knowledge with wisdom.

Focused on life in schools, our own policy research tells an "accountability story" that is much different from the narrative conveyed by the *accountability pillar*. Our concerns about the power that the "official" *pillar* seems to have in providing the account of how things are going in Alberta schools led to our early ideas for a collaborative project. The plan was to provide a space for educators to think outside or beyond prevailing discourses and, thus, to make space for alternative accountability narratives. The result was a graduate course, offered through the Department of Educational Policies Studies at the University of Alberta and held in conjunction with the Alberta Teachers' Association's spring 2008 symposium, *Leadership in Educational Accountability: Sustaining Professional Learning and Innovation in Alberta Schools.*

Most of the students in the course were K-12 school leaders enrolled in the Department's educational administration and leadership specialization, but students from across the Department's specializations in adult education, Indigenous Peoples education and theoretical, cultural and international studies in education, and from the Faculty of Education's master of educational studies, also participated.

Through engaging with the symposium speakers, representatives of the province's various education partners and the course readings and discussions, students integrated ideas into their own examinations, analyses and critiques of a range of accountability issues and policies. Students wrote final papers that were thoughtful and insightful. Together, they represented the much needed context that was missing in the huge amount of literature written on the topic of educational accountability– the insights and reflections of the practitioner, as presented and interpreted *by* the practitioner.

Realizing that we could not include all of the students' papers, we had to make some difficult decisions about which would be selected. We read and reread the papers, as an editorial group, to discern which would "hang together" to relate the experiences of accountability from a range of positions and perspectives. The result is the present collection. This book is meant for all audiences interested in educational policy and a fresh take on what is happening in local sites in the name of accountability. Although written from particular locations, positions and perspectives, each chapter presents valuable insights into how prevailing notions about accountability have been interpreted and put into practice.

During the course's pre-symposium workshop and the Symposium, we had the good fortune and privilege of learning from Dr. Pasi Sahlberg, educator and school improvement activist. Pasi agreed to take the impressions and understandings that he gathered during his time with us and relate them to his own understandings and broad expertise about and experiences of educational accountability to write a chapter that could be included in this volume. As a result, we are pleased to have Pasi's chapter, *Learning First: School Accountability for a Sustainable Society* set the stage for our collection. Pasi explains that current accountability practices that place emphasis on standardized testing are not what is necessary for improving education. He cites evidence that high-stakes testing restricts creativity and innovation and, using Finland as an example, he offers suggestions for education policies that promote trust and collective responsibility in schools. Concluding with a discussion of the importance of intelligent accountability, Pasi provides ways to think about a kind of educational accountability that will contribute to a sustainable society.

In chapter 2, Shelley Willier argues that discussions of accountability in First Nations education cannot take place without knowing the educational legacy of the experiences, perspectives, hopes and disappointments of First Nations people. Through relating the information shared in oral histories of pre-contact conceptions of education and in the narratives of first-hand experiences of residential schools, Shelley provides the necessary background for appreciating the current landscape of First Nation education in many communities. By focusing on issues related to Alberta's new First Nations, Métis and Inuit (FNMI), *accountability pillar* policies and federal, provincial and First Nations involvement in educational provision, Shelley points to the contradictions that are apparent in projects meant to serve First Nations students. She argues that the Cree understandings of responsibility, relationship and community provide alternatives to current conceptions of accountability that might be more appropriate for transforming public education to meet the needs and goals of First Nations and all Albertans.

In Chapter 3, School Choice and Accountability: Alberta's Problematic Combination, Troy Davies argues that, in Alberta, policies for school choice and accountability work in concert to produce quasi-market effects. Specifically, he draws on research conducted in our province that suggests that, because school leaders are accountable in significant ways for increasing standardized test results and for attracting students, in at least one urban centre they endeavour to build the reputation of their schools through marketing strategies. Because the research asserts that it is not evident that these efforts increase student achievement or improve teaching and learning, Troy concludes with questions about whether the potential benefits of choice programs have become undermined by the ways in which accountability is tied to funding, and he reflects on how the school choice-accountability combination may be operating to distract us from some of the moral and democratic purposes of public education.

Patricia Gervais begins her chapter 4, *Accountability and the Individual Program Plan,* with an description of how the professional expertise, commitment and the high costs associated with the education of students with special needs results in a push and pull between the ethical-professional and economic-bureaucratic demands of educational accountability. Drawing on the history of inclusive education and the Individual Program Plan (IPP) in Alberta and on the findings of a recent research study that examined educators' understandings of the IPP, Patricia reveals why the IPP is a source of tension for teachers with special needs students in their classrooms. She suggests that, while teachers are more concerned with the ethical-professional dimensions of accountability, they spend a great deal of time attending to the economic-bureaucratic demands of accountability related to completing the IPP. In this sense, the IPP functions more as an accountability tool than it does as a learning document and it may be more of a distraction than it is a benefit to the education of children with exceptional needs.

In chapter 5, *Alleviating Teacher Alienation: Sustainable, Distributed Leadership and Capacity for Putting Accountability into Perspective,* Heather Kennedy-Plant points to alienation as a negative consequence of the pressures teachers experience while working within government-mandated accountability regimes. To define teacher alienation, she draws on the literature that describes the effects of a performance culture that is the product of recent educational reforms. She argues that decreased professional autonomy and intensification leave teachers feeling disconnected from what they value in their work. She argues that sustainable, distributed leadership offers the potential to alleviate teacher alienation through the development of both individual and organization capacity at the school level. This, she suggests, also strengthens possibilities for student learning and success.

Alanna Crawford begins her chapter 6, *Alberta's Distributed Learning Strategy and Implementation Plan: Impact on Learning, Student Support and Assessment* by outlining a framework that incorporates four "pillars" for answering the question, what is education? She employs this framework to examine Alberta's *Distributed Learning Strategy* as it relates to effective student support practices and partnerships among various educational stakeholders. Her chapter identifies some discrepancies between the *Strategy* and the principles of the four pillars of education. Alanna concludes by offering some considerations for meaningful implementation of innovative assessment practices for distributed learning.

In chapter 7, *Literacy, Accountability and Inclusive Education: Possibilities for Re-framing Alberta's Literacy Framework* Kelli Ewasiuk and Brenda L. Spencer focus on a pair of key policy documents that constitute the draft of a framework for literacy education in Alberta. Their detailed analysis reveals how policy alignment and policy coherence establish strong conceptions of both literacy education and accountability. Discourses of shared responsibility and accountability and for standardization and coherence promote "external coherence" and "top-down" accountability, which are at cross-purposes with the documents' other recommendations for process-oriented approaches to literacy education. Kelli and Brenda draw on some of the critiques of externally driven, results-oriented approaches to literacy learning, teaching and assessment to conclude with some suggestions for "internal coherence" and "holistic accountability" that might serve as alternative ideas for how literacy and accountability could be framed.

In chapter 8, Randy Hetherington makes the case that public education systems must operate on the basis of trust. He examines key relationships of Alberta's organizational structure to illustrate their complexity. He describes the position and role of the superintendent as pivotal to building cultures of trust and, therefore, to facilitating and mediating the accountability tensions that emerge the different organizational groups connect and their functions intersect. While the needs and demands of organizational and stakeholder groups are increasingly pressing, Randy argues that the superintendent must negotiate the paradox of the position – asserting authority and building trust. He draws on Pasi Sahlberg's (this volume; 2008) ideas about "intelligent accountability" to forward his argument that a strong culture of trust can support positive change in public education systems.

Finally, Darren Krasowski, in chapter 9, *Product-centred and Process-centre Approaches, and Possibilities for an Alternative Accountability Framework,* argues that the challenges related to the implementation of various accountability models and programs for public education originate in the tensions between what he refers to as product-centred and process-centred approaches to accountability. Darren describes these approaches in detail, highlighting the ways in which they are employed together even though they are often contradictory. He analyzes Alberta's current accountability framework and argues that it places too much weight on a product-centred approach. He suggests a compromise between the product- and process-centred approaches and, by drawing on Pasi Sahlberg's work (this volume; 2007; 2008), he proposes a model similar to the one upon which the Finnish K-12 education system is based. He offers recommendations for a new conceptualization of an accountability framework that encourages the appropriate use of summative assessment data and that recognizes the importance of the professional judgement of classroom teachers.

Together, the chapters of this book offer insights into the complexity and difficulty of achieving the goals of accountability policies and programs while, at the same time, attending to the often-competing purposes and aims of public education. Moreover, these chapters are narratives of the kind that do not get told by the "empirical stories" presented in the form of "score cards" of and for accountability that seemingly dominate our own educational context. Indeed, they offer a comprehensive set of ideas for thinking about, discussing and debating issues of accountability– what it means, what it does, and what it ought to look like in public education settings. We think you'll find the collection both interesting and provocative!

NOTES

[1] For example, the Key Partners on Educational Accountability in Alberta working group was established in 2006 by the Alberta Teachers' Association for the purpose of examining the province's accountability framework and making recommendations to the Ministry of Education. The group included members of various provincial organizations representing trustees, superintendents, faculties of education and school councils. We served on this committee as the representatives of the University of Alberta and the Alberta Teachers' Association.

REFERENCES

Alberta Education. (2009a). *Accountability in Alberta's education system.* Retrieved February 19, 2009, from http://www.education.alberta.ca/admin/funding/accountability.aspx

Alberta Education. (2009b). *How the accountability pillar works.* Retrieved February 19, 2009, from http://www.education.alberta.ca/admin/funding/accountability/works.aspx

Lessard, C., & Brassard, A. (2005, April). *Educational governance in Canada: Trends and significance.* Paper presented at the American Educational Research Association 2005 annual meeting, Montréal, PQ.

McNeil, L. M. (1986). *Contradictions of control: School structure and knowledge.* New York: Routledge & K. Paul.

Sahlberg, P. (2007). Education policies for raising student learning: The Finnish approach. *Journal of Education Policy, 22*(2), 147–171.

Sahlberg, P. (2008). *From periphery to limelight: Educational change in Finland.* Unpublished manuscript.

PASI SAHLBERG

1. LEARNING FIRST

School Accountability for a Sustainable Society

GLOBAL INFECTIONS AND RANDOM CURES

Most countries, among them those on the top of the international educational rankings, are reforming their education systems to provide their citizens with knowledge and skills that enable them to engage actively in democratic societies and dynamic, knowledge-based economies. These initiatives are further driven by recent educational reviews that show how some cities, provinces and countries have better education than others. For example, Singapore, Alberta, Finland and Cuba have been mentioned among those jurisdictions where students do better on tests, are more likely to complete their education on time and tend to stay in formal education longer than their peers elsewhere (Carnoy, 2007; OECD, 2007b; Sahlberg, 2007; Schleicher, 2006). Interestingly, these educational systems have used different policies, and sometimes even contrary reforms, to achieve good educational performance.

Rather than shifting emphasis towards standardized knowledge of content and mastery of routine skills, some advanced education systems are focusing on flexibility, risk-taking, creativity and problem solving through modern methods of teaching, such as co-operative learning, and through the use of multilateral clusters, community networks and ICT in teaching. The number of examples is increasing, including China, a burgeoning economic power that is loosening its standardized control on education by making a school-based curriculum a national policy priority. Japan and Singapore are adopting the idea of "less is more" in teaching in order to make room for creativity and innovation. Even in England, the most test-intensive region in the world, the government is putting an end to all standardized testing in secondary schools. As a reaction to the overemphasis on knowledge-based teaching and test-based accountability, authorities in Japan, Singapore and some countries of the European Union are developing more dynamic forms of curriculum, introducing more intelligent forms of assessment and accountability and enhancing sustainable leadership in education in order to find alternative instructional approaches that promote the productive learning required in knowledge economies. Instead of focusing on single institutions, education reforms are beginning to encourage clustering of schools and communities. At the core of this idea is *complementarity*, i.e. co-operation between and striving for better learning in the cluster. Clustering and networking also

K.D. Gariepy, B.L. Spencer and J.-C. Couture (eds.), Educational Accountability:
Professional Voices From the Field, 1–22.

appear to be core factors in nations' economic competitiveness and efforts to cope with globalization.

Indeed, globalization is a cultural paradox: it simultaneously unifies and diversifies people and cultures. It unifies national education policies by integrating them with broader global trends. Because problems and challenges are similar from one education system to the next, solutions and education reform agendas are also becoming similar. Due to international benchmarking of education systems by using common indicators and the international comparisons of student achievement, the distinguishing features of different education systems are becoming more visible. For example, the OECD's *Programme for International Student Assessment* (PISA) has mobilized scores of education experts to visit other countries in order to learn how to redefine their own education policies. However, globalization has also accelerated international collaboration, exchange of ideas and transfer of education policies between education systems (Carnoy, 1999; Levin, 2001). Analyzing global policy developments and education reforms has become a common practice in many ministries of education, development agencies and regional administrations. Therefore, the world's education systems inevitably share some core values, functions and structures. The question arises whether increased global interaction among policy-makers and educators, especially benchmarking of education systems through agreed indicators and borrowing and lending educational policies, has promoted common approaches to education reform throughout the world.

Although improvement of education systems is a global phenomenon, there is no reliable, recent comparative analysis about how education reforms in different countries have been designed and implemented. However, the professional literature indicates that the focus on educational development has shifted from structural reforms to improving the quality and relevance of education (Hargreaves & Goodson, 2006; Sahlberg, 2007). As a result, curriculum development, student assessment, teacher evaluation, integration of information and communication technologies into teaching and learning, proficiency in basic competencies (i.e., reading and writing) and mathematical and scientific literacy have become common priorities in education reforms around the world (Hargreaves & Shirley, in press). I have called this the *Global Educational Reform Movement (GERM)*.

The inspiration for the emergence of the GERM comes from three primary sources. The first is the new paradigm of learning that became dominant in the 1980s. The breakthrough of cognitive and constructivist approaches to learning gradually shifted the focus of education reforms from teaching to learning. According to this paradigm, intended outcomes of schooling emphasize greater conceptual understanding, problem-solving, emotional and multiple intelligences and interpersonal skills, rather than the memorization of facts or the mastery of irrelevant skills. At the same time, however, the need for proficiency in literacy and numeracy has also become a prime target of education reforms. The second inspiration is the public demand for guaranteed, effective learning for all pupils. Inclusive education arrangements and the introduction of common learning standards for all have been offered as means to promote the ideal of education for all. The third inspiration is the accountability movement in education that has accompanied the global wave of decentralization of public services. Making schools and teachers accountable for their work has led to the introduction of education standards, indicators and benchmarks for teaching and learning, aligned assessments and testing and prescribed curricula. As Popham (2007) has noted, various forms of test-based accountability have emerged where school performance and raising the quality of education are closely tied to the processes of accreditation, promotion, sanctions and financing.

The GERM has had significant consequences for teachers' work and students' learning in schools. Because this agenda promises significant gains in efficiency and quality of education, it has been widely accepted as a basic ideology of change, both politically and professionally. Table 1 describes some effects that the GERM has had and is having in schools, especially on teaching and learning (Hargreaves 2003; Hargreaves & Fink, 2005; Sahlberg, 2006; 2007). It also identifies alternative reform principles that have been adopted in places such as the Nordic countries.

Table 1. Some global features of education development and their alternatives since the early 1980s.

Education Policies and Reform Principles	
Global Education Reform Movement (GERM)	*Alternative Reform Movement (ARM)*
Strict Standards	**Loose Standards**
Setting clear, high, centrally prescribed performance standards for all schools, teachers and students to improve the quality and equity of outcomes.	Setting clear but flexible national framework for school-based curriculum planning. Encouraging local solutions to national goals in order to find best ways to create optimal learning opportunities for all.
Focus on Literacy and Numeracy	**Focus on Broad and Deep Learning**
Basic knowledge and skills in reading, writing, mathematics and the natural sciences serve as prime targets of education reform.	Teaching and learning focus on deep, broad learning, giving equal value to all aspects of the growth of an individual's personality, moral character, creativity, knowledge and skills.
Teaching for Predetermined Results	**Encouraging Risk-taking and Creativity**
Reaching higher standards as criterion for success and good performance; minimizes educational risk-taking; narrows teaching to content and use of methods beneficial to attaining preset results.	School-based and teacher-owned curricula facilitate finding novel approaches to teaching and learning, hence encouraging risk-taking and uncertainty in leadership, teaching and learning.

Transferring External Innovations for Educational Revolutions	Learning from the Past and Respecting Pedagogical Conservatism
Sources of educational change are external innovations brought to schools and teachers through legislation or national programs. These often replace existing improvement strategies.	Teaching honours traditional pedagogical values, such as teacher's role and relationship with students. Main sources of school improvement are proven good practices from the past.

Test-based Accountability	Responsibility and Trust
School performance and raising student achievement are closely tied to processes of promotion, inspection and rewarding schools and teachers. Winners normally gain fiscal rewards whereas struggling schools and individuals are punished.	Gradual building of a culture of responsibility and trust within the education system that ultimately values teacher and principal professionalism in judging what is best for students and in reporting their learning progress. Targeting resources and support to schools and students who are at risk to fail or to be left behind.

The GERM emphasizes some fundamental new orientations to learning and educational administration. It suggests three strong directions to improve quality, equity and effectiveness of education: putting priority on learning, aiming at good learning achievement for all students and making assessment an integral part of the teaching and learning process. However, it also strengthens market-like logic and procedures in education. First and most importantly, the GERM assumes that external performance standards, describing what teachers should teach and what students should do and learn, lead to better learning for all. By concentrating on the basics and defining explicit learning targets for students and teachers, such standards place strong emphases on mastering the core skills of reading, writing, mathematical and scientific literacy. Second, the GERM assumes that the most effective way to improve education systems is to bring well-developed innovations to schools and classrooms. Systematic training of teachers and staff is an essential element of this approach. Third, the GERM relies on an assumption that competition between schools, teachers and students is the most productive way to raise the quality of education. This requires that parents can choose schools for their children, that schools have enough autonomy and that schools and teachers are held accountable for their students' learning.

A sustainable society is grounded upon the power to think, learn and innovate. It depends equally on individual and collective ways of doing these things. Learning to think, to learn and to innovate requires more than orderly implementation of externally mandated regulations. Learning together, creating new ideas and learning to live with other people peacefully, all high-demand features of modern schooling, best occur in an environment decidedly different from what some of our schools offer young people and their teachers today. Furthermore, treating ingenuity and diversity simultaneously in classrooms is a challenge for teachers. Schools will not be able to meet these expectations to educate their students for a sustainable society unless they have:

- internal conditions that respect their professional intuition, knowledge and skills to craft the best learning environments for their students;
- social context and necessary social capital in their communities that provide encouraging and supportive conditions for learning; and
- adequate external norms and expectations that rely on responsibility and internal accountability to reach good learning for all students.

The purpose of this chapter is to stress the distinction between intelligent and non-intelligent education policies– especially those addressing learning and accountability– and how they direct teachers and students toward learning differently. The primary assumption is that students and teachers should have clear responsibilities regarding their work in schools. In other words, certain school accountability is needed but it should be designed and put into practice wisely. Due to the failure to do that, schools in many countries have an emerging educational dilemma: How to deal with external productivity demands and teaching for a sustainable society with moral purpose, simultaneously?

THE COEXISTENCE DILEMMA: COLLABORATION AND COMPETITION

Competitive pressures in the forms of higher productivity, better efficiency and system-wide excellence are affecting schools and teachers. Competition over students and financial resources are shifting schools' *modi operandi* from those based on moral purpose to those based on productivity and efficiency, i.e. measurable outcomes, higher test scores and better positions in school league tables. Indeed, increasing public-sector productivity is changing small, personalised schools into larger institutions characterized by opportunity and choice, but rarely by personal care and collective social and human responsibility. Market-like efficiency measures have brought standards, testing and the race for higher achievement, as measured by tests, to the centre of teachers' and students' lives, both inside and outside school. All these are a threat to social capital in schools and communities. Indeed, schools are viewed as necessary elements for exponential economic growth in the service of wealth accumulation in the knowledge economy. Many education strategies of today seem to take for granted that the new educational order, through standards and test-based accountability, will best serve this purpose; however, what the world and its people need is not unbridled wealth accumulation and a population programmed by schools to want it. Rather, we need education that critically examines the implications of this phase of history, which Rees (2003) sees as the last for retaining an ecosystem in sustainable balance and which Sachs (2008) argues requires a new form of international cooperation. Education has a key role to play in accomplishing both of these. Therefore, teaching in a sustainable society must be wisely balanced between the different expectations described here.

Teaching is a profession that is typically driven by ethical motives or intrinsic desire, just as nursing, the performing arts and humanitarian services. Most teachers, therefore, expect to teach in congruence with their moral purpose, i.e. so that students can understand and learn to promote their personal development and growth, not just for favourable exam scores or other externally set conditions of progress. Helping other people, and thereby one's own community and society, is the basic element of moral purpose associated with the teaching profession. Teachers are, by their nature, important facilitators in building social capital within their communities and nations. Therefore, teachers historically have a broader professional work focus than just academic learning or technical skill development, as reported by Lortie (1975) and Hargreaves (2008), for example. Increased emphasis on knowledge testing and competition has left many teachers "hugging the middle," as Cuban (2007) puts it. Teachers try to balance their work between the moral purpose of student-centred pedagogy within education as a public right on one hand, and the drive for higher standards through the perceived efficiency of the presentation-recitation mode of instruction within the perspective of education as a private good, on the other.

In this chapter, I argue that test-based accountability policies have put teachers between schooling for moral purpose with student-centred pedagogy and worthwhile learning on one side, and efficiency-driven education with teacher-centred instruction and achievement on the other. Students, as the main recipients of schooling, must balance fulfilling their own aspirations with external demands for performance that are often not only conflicting, but also unethical and contradictory.

Steering education systems towards producing intended outcomes requires congruence between teaching for the knowledge economy and what education reforms are expecting from teachers and students. In some cases, however, what schools are explicitly or implicitly assumed to do to improve their performance within ongoing education reforms contradicts what is needed from schools to support economic competitiveness. Comparison of these two change forces at the level of education systems, schools and classroom indicates some difficult incompatibilities and controversies. At the macro level, economic competitiveness demands an education system flexible enough to be able to react to weak signals and to produce a coordinated and collaborative response. Such a reaction and response is made possible by sustainable leadership. An education system's flexibility is promoted by freedom of choice, decentralized management and a culture of trust in professional communities, i.e. teachers and educational leaders. At the same time, education reforms are equipping education systems with standards and regulations that set the criteria and targets for success and measurement. These education standards aim at raising the expectations of teaching and learning by specifying what every student should know and be able to do. At the school level, economic competitiveness needs the organization of work to enable alternative scheduling, integration of subjects and increased teacher collaboration. Creativity is promoted by using a wide spectrum of teaching methods, such as co-operative learning, simulations, role-play and group investigation, and building bridges between the school and the community. Due to global education reforms, however, work in schools is influenced by prescribed curricula that are often used to determine the performance level and, mistakenly, the quality of schools. Teachers tend to rely on traditional teaching arrangements and methods in order to minimize the risk of failure. Finally, teaching and learning for more competitive economies requires teachers and students to work together in safe and stimulating learning environments that focus on broad learning objectives, encourage everyone to participate and use alternative approaches to achieve goals. Risk-taking in teaching and learning is promoted by co-operative cultures, mutual trust and feedback that recognize students' efforts as well as attainment. Dream or vision is a source of emotional energy that is a necessary driver of change.

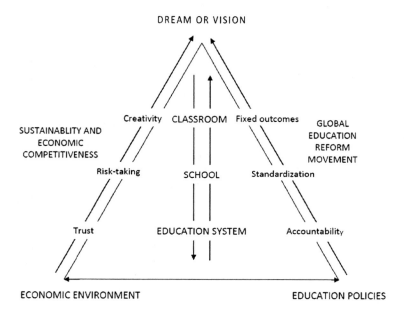

Figure 1. Key factors of economic competitiveness and education reform (Sahlberg, 2006)

As a result of typical education reforms, however, teaching and learning are often characterized by stress and fear as the focus is on being successful in achieving the predetermined learning standards. Therefore, students primarily learn alone rather than co-operatively in small groups, in order to minimize personal risks. Open and alternative teaching methods and task designs are not favoured. Figure 1 summarizes the comparison of sustainability and competitiveness *vis-a-vis* the global education reform movement mentioned above. It also calls for coexistence of collaboration and competition.

TEST-BASED ACCOUNTABILITY AND BROKEN DREAMS OF LEARNING

The GERM approach to educational change is based on a belief in competition and information as the key drivers of educational improvement. This approach combines two traditions in public education that have previously been only loosely connected, namely, public accountability and student testing. During the past twenty years, test-based accountability has held schools, teachers and students increasingly accountable for learning as measured by knowledge tests (Carnoy, Elmore & Siskin, 2003; Hamilton, Stecher & Klein, 2002; Ben Jaafar & Anderson,

2007; Ladd and Fiske, 2003; Popham, 2007). In their analysis of the Education Reform Act 1988 of England, Levin and Fullan (2008) summarize the logic of market-driven educational change as:
- The belief that competition in the economy as a whole drives efficiency and improvement could be applied to schools as well, so that competition among schools would lead to better outcomes for students.
- In order for schools to compete, individual schools would require much more autonomy.
- Parents would need to be able to choose the schools their children attended.
- In order to choose, parents and the public would require comparable measures of student achievement and education quality for all schools, based on a single national curriculum. (pp. 289-290)

The incentive-based educational reform movement has stimulated enormous debates between and within education and policy-making communities during the last two decades. Research-generated evidence on school accountability is rather difficult to interpret. The key question is: "Do students perform better in competition-based school systems that have choice, autonomy and accountability measures in place?" Proponents of greater accountability contend that competition improves student learning by heightening incentives for teachers and students to try harder and do better. Accountability systems typically combine clear performance standards, external monitoring and testing of results, and consequential rewards and sanctions to promote competition between schools and individuals. Therefore, accountability advocates argue that by generating better information on student performance, such systems indirectly benefit students, teachers and principals in their efforts to achieve the best possible outcomes. Moreover, proponents claim that school autonomy, often an element of accountability systems, replaces the rigidity and bureaucracy of centralized governance with creativity and efficiency of local leadership (Wössmann, Lüdemann, Schütz & West, 2007). Competition among students due to free choice of schools, supporters say, releases energy and promotes school improvement as financial resources follow the students.

Some of the recent studies also suggest that with respect to accountability, "students perform better where policies are in place that aim at students (external exit exams), teachers (monitoring of lessons), and schools (assessment-based comparisons)" (Wössmann et al., 2007, p. 4). A study by Carnoy and Loeb (2002) of the effects of external accountability on student outcomes in the 50 states of the USA revealed that "students in high-accountability states averaged significantly greater gains on the NAEP 8th-grade math test than students in states with little or no state measures to improve student performance" (p. 305). Furthermore, their study concludes that students in high-accountability states do not display significantly higher retention or lower high school completion rates. A 2006 OECD PISA study covering 57 nations also indicates that accountability, autonomy and choice are positively associated with the level of student achievement across nations (OECD, 2007a). This study, however, does not discuss the types of accountability policies in participating education systems.

Competition as an approach to raising the quality and improving equity of education has indeed a lot of common sense: the most important justification for success of the school is, and should be, whether students have learned what they were expected to learn. The expansion of the global educational testing industry has brought along optimism suggesting that it is possible to find out, with sufficient precision, what students have learned by testing them. "Unfortunately," Popham writes, "the tests currently being used as the centrepiece of the test-based accountability are the wrong ones" (Popham, 2007, p. 166). Today's accountability tests do not measure what teachers taught to students; instead, they measure "what those students brought to schools" (Popham, 2007, p. 167). Test-based accountability policies that rely on flawed tests can harm schools, rather than help them to improve. Other critical researchers (Au, 2008; McNeil, 2000; Sacks, 2001) add that the cost of test-based accountability systems is too high and the tools currently used too weak to justify permanent change or promote worthwhile learning in schools. The problem, actually, is not necessarily holding students, teachers and schools accountable *per se*, but rather how accountability is arranged and practiced. Whenever educational accountability relies chiefly on low quality knowledge tests, it can be made to work better by employing more appropriate tests and other assessment models that complement the information gathered through such tests.

Part of the opposition to test-based accountability comes from individuals and institutions who fear that the business-like management of education, with its in-built high-stakes testing and consequential accountability, will eventually harm the quality, equity and overall viability of public education as it is today (Au, 2008; Hargreaves, 2008; Ladd & Fiske, 2003; Nichols & Berliner, 2007; Popham, 2007; Sacks, 2001). Others contend that the accountability movement, with increased competition, will not improve quality of schools and learning. Indeed, it is creating adverse effects, such as narrowing of learning, demoralizing teachers, increasing student drop-outs and loosening integrity among school administrators, teachers and students (McNeil, Coppola, Radigan & Vasquez Heilig, 2008). High-stakes testing systems are, according to a growing number of researchers, including Au (2007), Berry and Sahlberg (2006), Nichols and Berliner (2007), Loeb, Knapp and Elfers (2008), and Shirley (2008), narrowing curricula, increasing the practice of presentation-recitation instructional modes, stifling creativity and undermining student engagement in schools. This has led to acts of civil disobedience. Recently, for example, a science teacher in Seattle was suspended for refusing to administer a state-mandated test in his classroom. He crystallized his motive by saying that "all we have to do is have faith in these kids and work as hard as we can with these kids and their families and they're going to do fine" ("Teacher Suspended for Refusing to Give State Test," 2008).

In an international review for the OECD, Wössmann et al. (2007) stressed that according to some critics, "choice and competition in schooling will hurt the most disadvantaged, thereby weaken[ing] social cohesion" (p. 10). Good schools in open, competition-driven educational markets will only accept the best students, leaving behind those who are most in need of attention and care. Nichols and Berliner (2007) offer an even gloomier view of education as a consequence of strengthened, test-based accountability. With reference to Campbell's law, which states that "the more any quantitative social indicator is used for social decision-making, the more subject it will be to corruption pressures and the more apt it will be to distort and corrupt the social processes it is intended to monitor," they report that over-reliance on high-stakes testing exerts serious, negative repercussions at every level of the public school system. Excluding weaker students from tests, cheating by students and administrators and systemic corruption are already found in many schools and districts as "survival responses" to increased testing and the race for resources and fame.

An emerging concern is that current, externally-mandated, test-based account-ability structures in public education have become increasingly narrowed, and as mentioned earlier, focusing almost solely on standardized knowledge tests and the publishing of results. Testing-driven systems often ignore the moral purposes of schooling and thereby fail to consider such antecedents as curriculum development, school and classroom leadership and school–community contexts. As Tschannen-Moran (2007) points out, the challenges associated with achieving new and higher social expectations of learning and equity in schools have led to suspicion of teachers and schools. Higher standards and greater accountability, she says, "have fostered conditions of distrust and blame" (p. 100). The presence of trust does not guarantee improved educational performance, but its absence signals failure.

THE EMERGENCE OF SCHOOL-FRIENDLY ACCOUNTABILITY

Rather than insisting on abolishing school accountability systems, there is a need for a new type of accountability policy that balances qualitative and quantitative measures, and that builds on mutual accountability, professional responsibility and trust. This is often termed intelligent accountability (Sahlberg, 2007; Secondary School Heads Association, 2003). This framework ensures that schools work effectively and efficiently toward both the public good and the development of students. Intelligent accountability utilizes a wide variety of data that gives genuine expression to strengths and weaknesses of a particular school in meeting its goals. It combines internal accountability, consisting of school processes, self-evaluations, critical reflection and school-community interaction, with levels of external accountability that build on monitoring, sample-based student assessment and thematic evaluations appropriate to the status of development of each individual school.

Intelligent accountability respects the complexity of human and organizational learning. It also stresses the principle of mutual responsibility. This means that accountability dynamics can be regarded as a two-way arrow. On one hand, schools should be held accountable to decision makers and the community for the overall outcomes of schooling. These outcomes, collectively defined by the school and their community stakeholders, go far beyond student achievement results that remain the focus of external, standardized tests. Expected outcomes include non-cognitive areas, such as social skills, moral values and aspects of personality not assessed by current tests. On the other hand, decision makers, authorities and school boards should also be held accountable for providing schools and their students, teachers and principals with the resources, conditions and opportunities needed to attain jointly agreed-upon educational goals.

School, as a social organization, many have argued, has traditionally been a place for cultivating and caring for trust and responsible behaviours (Hargreaves, 2003; Sharan and Chin Tan, 2008). Learning to be responsible for one's own and others' well-being and growth is a tacit goal of schools. Societies with high social capital often also have higher mutual trust in other people. In such societies, as Hargreaves (2008) suggests, responsibility precedes accountability; in other words, accountability is the remainder that is left when responsibility is subtracted. Responsibility grows from trust. Institutional cultures based on trust also spread responsibility across their people. One may also note that when trust disappears, so does an individual's sense of accountability, or responsibility – and vice versa. Therefore, building trust within schools and especially among schools and their communities, is a crucial step toward intelligent accountability and stronger mutual responsibility for our school systems. Unfortunately, in many schools, external policies have replaced responsibility and trust with accountability, which has left them stuck in the middle when reaching out for their moral purpose and material rewards.

Part of the challenge to transform current accountability policies into more intelligent ones is the narrow and flawed ways of collecting information that are used in accountability judgements. The most commonly used instruments are data from standardized tests and examinations, which typically focus on knowledge rather than meta-cognitive skills, and which often try to cover too many aspects of curriculum, rather than concentrating on the essentials. Alternative systems of accountability, as suggested by Nichols and Berliner (2007) and Popham (2007), for example, should shift the focus from assessment *of* learning to assessment *for* learning, and employ different methods of assessment, including performance tests (e.g. portfolios and projects evaluated by judges). This, of course, is closely related to the level of trust: Can we rely also on teachers' judgment about how their students are learning, just like we normally trust the verdict of a court judge or diagnosis of a medical doctor?

Currently, data are normally collected through a comprehensive census applied to all schools and all students of the age cohort. This is both expensive and not the most appropriate strategy to learn how educational systems are progressing. Census-based, external assessments also often ignore the peculiarities and profiles that individual schools have as a result of their own curricula. As in many other cases, it is not necessary to ensure school accountability through a census. Alternatively, it can be achieved more easily and equally reliably through a statistical sample. The logic of using samples rather than a census is simple: In health checks, it is quite enough to use samples of blood that appear to be adequate to inform both the physician and the patient of state of health! The physician does not need to check all the blood to make her diagnosis. Many governments, however, rely on educational accountability by census, although it has evident drawbacks: it is expensive, shifts focus away from worthwhile learning and is subject to widespread, immoral abuse and collateral damage (Jones, Jones & Hargrove, 2003; Nichols & Berliner, 2007; Sacks, 2001). Currently used knowledge tests, as Popham (2007) eloquently claims, are not good enough to allow teachers to use them to improve their teaching. The high-stakes, test-based accountability systems implemented in many nations create, therefore, a conflict between a spirit of risk-taking and creativity – essential elements of teaching and learning for the knowledge society – and normative pedagogies determined by the reach for better test scores.

THE FINNISH MODEL: QUALITY, EQUITY
AND TRUST – ALL AT REASONABLE COST

In this chapter, I have so far conveyed my concern that tightened, test-based accountability for schools, teachers and students may jeopardize schools' efforts to teach for the knowledge society and a sustainable future, and is not, therefore, the best way to improve learning in schools. Finland is an example of a nation that has demonstrated both steady educational progress since early 1970s and built an equitable educational system operating in good congruence with a competitive knowledge economy (Aho, Pitkänen & Sahlberg, 2006; Hargreaves, Halasz & Pont, 2008; Sahlberg, 2007; 2009). It is therefore reasonable to look at how Finland has addressed the global demand for stronger, test-based accountability in its educational system.

Interestingly, the term *accountability* cannot be found in Finnish educational policy discourse. Educational reform principles since early 1990s, when much of public sector administration went through decentralization, have relied on building professional responsibilities within schools, rather than applying external accountability structures and encouraging lateral capacity building among schools. Therefore, sample-based testing, thematic assessments, reflective self-evaluations and putting learning first have established a culture of mutual responsibilities and trust. For example, before the end of upper-secondary school (or grade 12), no external, high-stakes tests are employed. Moreover, there is no inspection of teachers and only loose external standards steering the schools. This leaves teachers with good opportunities, as well as the professional responsibility, to focus on learning with their students, rather than being concerned about frequent testing and public rankings of their schools. Some policy makers predicted in the mid-1990s that Finland would follow the school accountability policies carried out by the global educational reform movement; however, in a review of policy development in Finland ten years later, test-based accountability is not even mentioned (Itkonen & Jahnukainen, 2007; Laukkanen, 1998; 2008).

As Finland attracts global attention due to its high-performing education system, it is worth asking about progress made since the 1980s. If progress can be reliably identified, then the question becomes: What factors might be behind successful education reform? In my recent analysis of educational reform policies in Finland (Sahlberg, 2007), I describe how Finland changed its traditional education system, with little to celebrate in terms of international comparisons, into a model of a modern, publicly financed education system with widespread equity, good quality and large participation, all at a reasonable cost (OECD, 2007b; Sahlberg, 2007; Schleicher, 2006). What is significant from this analysis is the steady progress made during the past three decades in four main domains: (1) increased levels of educational attainment of the adult population, (2) widespread equity, (3) a good level of student learning, and (4) moderate overall spending, almost solely from public sources. Before describing the educational changes since the 1970s, I will briefly summarize the main elements determining the level of Finnish educational system performance.

First, there has been a steady growth in participation in all levels of education in Finland since 1970. The growth was especially rapid in the upper-secondary education sector in the 1980s and, then, within the tertiary and adult education sectors in the 1990s, up to the present. Education policies that have driven Finnish reform since 1970 have prioritized creating equal opportunities, raising quality and increasing participation in all educational levels across Finnish society. More than 99% of the age cohort successfully complete compulsory basic education, about 95% continue their education in upper secondary schools or in the 10th grade of basic school (some 3%) immediately after graduation, and 90% of those starting upper secondary school eventually receive their school leaving certification, providing access to tertiary education (Statistics Finland, 2007). Two thirds of those enrol either in academic universities or professionally oriented polytechnics. Finally, over 50% of the Finnish adult population participates in adult-education programs. What is significant in this expansion of participation in education is that it has taken place without shifting the burden of costs to students or their parents. According to recent global education indicators, only 2% of Finnish expenditure on educational institutions is from private sources, compared to an OECD average of 13% (OECD, 2007b). Overall progress since 1970 in educational attainment by the Finnish adult population (15 years and older) is shown in Figure 2. The current situation is congruent with a typical profile of the human capital pyramid in advanced knowledge economies.

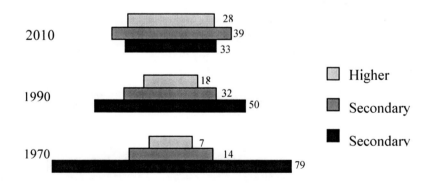

Figure 2. Level of educational attainment among the Finnish adult population (15 years and older) since 1970 as a proportion of basic, secondary and higher education qualification holders. Figures for 2010 are estimates (Sahlberg, 2009).

Second, education opportunities and, therefore, good learning outcomes, have spread rather evenly across Finland. There was a visible achievement gap among young adults at the start of comprehensive school in the early 1970s due to very different educational orientations associated with the old parallel system (Aho et al., 2006). This knowledge gap strongly corresponded with the socio-economic divide within Finnish society at that time. Although students' learning outcomes began to even out by the mid-1980s, streaming through ability grouping in mathematics and foreign languages kept the achievement gap relatively wide. After abolishing streaming in comprehensive school in the mid-1980s and making learning expectations similar for all students, the achievement gap between low and high achievers began to decrease. First evidence of this came from the OECD's PISA survey in 2000. Finland had one of the smallest performance variations between schools: less than one tenth of that variation in Japan, in reading literacy between schools of all OECD nations. A similar trend continued in the 2003 PISA cycle in mathematics and was strengthened in 2006 (OECD, 2001; 2004; 2007a). Figure 3 illustrates performance variance within and between schools in different OECD nations as assessed by the science scale in the 2006 PISA survey.

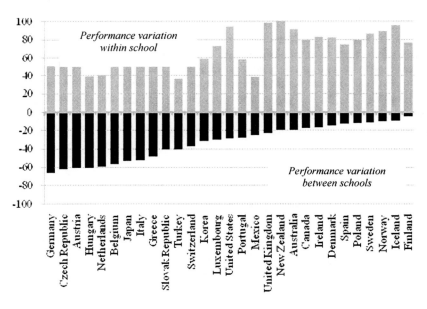

Figure 3. National variance within and between schools in student science performance in the 2006 PISA cycle (OECD, 2007a).

According to Figure 3, Finland has less than 5% between-school variance on the PISA science scale, whereas the average between-school variance in other OECD nations is about 33%. The fact that almost all Finnish inequality is within schools, as shown in Figure 3, means that the remaining differences are probably mostly due to variation in students' natural talent. Accordingly, variation between schools mostly relates to social inequality. Since this is a small source of variation in

Finland, it suggests that schools successfully deal with social inequality. This also indicates, as Grubb (2007) observed, that Finnish educational reform has succeeded in building an equitable education system in a relatively short time, a main objective of Finland's education reform agenda set in the early 1970s.

Third, Finnish students' learning is at a high international level, as determined by recent comparative student achievement studies. Although it is difficult to compare students' learning outcomes today with those of 1980, some evidence can be offered using International Educational Assessment (IEA) and OECD PISA surveys since the 1980s (Kupari & Välijärvi, 2005; Martin, Mullis, Gonzales, Gregory, Smith, Chrostowski, Garden & O'Connor, 2000; OECD, 2001; Robitaille & Garden, 1989). Based on these data, I reported elsewhere a summary of Finnish students' mathematics performance since 1981 compared to their peers in other countries (Sahlberg, 2007). The studies used include the Second International Mathematics Study (SIMS) in 1981 (8th grade, 20 nations), Trends in Mathematics and Science Study (TIMSS-R) in 1999 (8th grade, 38 nations) and the OECD PISA survey in 2000 (15-year olds, all 30 OECD member countries). These are the international student assessments surveys in which Finland participated since 1980. Since the nations participating in each international survey are not the same and the methodology of IEA and OECD surveys is different, the international average as a benchmarking value does not always provide a fully comparable or coherent picture.

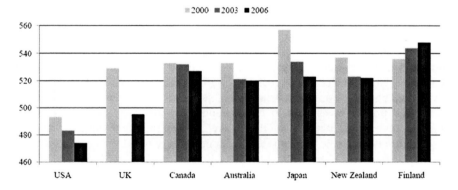

Figure 4. Finnish 15-year old students' performance in mathematics in three OECD PISA surveys between 2000 and 2006, compared to the performance of students in selected OECD countries.

Figure 4 shows another divergence in Finnish students' learning performance trends, as measured by the OECD PISA mathematics scale and in comparison to some OECD countries, over time. It is remarkable that student achievement in mathematics shows progress in Finland, contrary to many other education super powers. There is an increasing debate over what these international tests really measure, and it is beyond the scope of this chapter to discuss those issues or the validity of these studies. Criticism and proponents' arguments are available, for example, in Adams (2003), Bautier and Rayon (2007), Goldstein (2004), Nagy (1996), Prais (2003; 2004), Riley and Torrance (2003) and Schleicher (2006).

The OECD's PISA is increasingly being adopted as a global measure to benchmark nations' student achievement at the end of compulsory education. In 2006, the third cycle of this global survey was conducted in all 30 OECD member countries and in 27 other countries. It focuses on

> young people's ability to use their knowledge and skills to meet real-life challenges. This orientation reflects a change in the goals and objectives of curricula themselves, which are increasingly concerned with what students can do with what they learn at school and not merely with whether they have mastered specific curricular content. (OECD 2007a, p. 16).

In the 2006 PISA survey, Finland maintained its high performance in all assessed areas of student achievement. In science, the main focus of the survey, Finnish students outperformed their peers in all 56 countries. Furthermore, the first three PISA survey cycles since 2000 also indicate that Finnish educational performance is consistent over all assessed educational domains, and that Finnish students, on average, score highly in every survey across all subjects – in mathematics, science and reading literacy.

It seems that Finland has been able to reform its education system by increasing participation at all levels, making good education achievable to a large proportion of its population, and attaining comparatively high learning outcomes in most schools throughout the nation. All of this has been accomplished by financing education, including tertiary and adult education, almost exclusively from public sources. One more question regarding good educational performance remains to be addressed: How much does it cost the Finnish taxpayers? In OECD nations for which data on comparable trends are available for all educational levels combined, public and private investment in Finnish education increased 34% from 1995 to 2004 in real terms, while the OECD average for the same period was 42%. Expenditure on educational institutions as a percentage of GDP in Finland is at the OECD average, 6.1% in 2004 (OECD, 2007b). Less than 2% of total Finnish expenditure on education institutions comes from private sources. Figure 5 summarizes students' mean performance on the PISA science scale in relation to educational spending per student in 2006. These data indicate that good educational performance in Finland has been attained at reasonable cost.

Finnish educational success has encouraged people to search for causes of such favourable international performance. Most visitors to Finland discover elegant school buildings filled with calm children and highly educated teachers. They also recognise the broad autonomy that schools enjoy, the lack of interference from central education administration in schools' everyday activities, the systematic methods used to address problems in the lives of students, and the targeted, professional help available for those in need. Much of this may be helpful to visitors in benchmarking their own country's practice in relation to a leading education nation such as Finland. However, much of the secret of Finland's educational success remains undiscovered: What has the educational change process been like? What was done behind the scenes when key decisions were made to make that success possible? How much did Finnish educators take note of global education reform movements in creating their own approaches? What is the role of other public sector policies in making education system work so well?

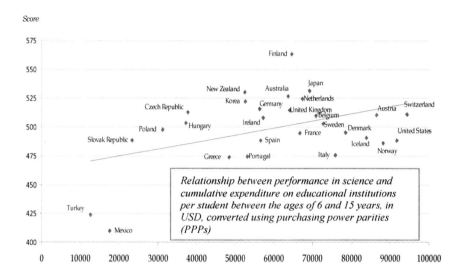

Figure 5. Student performance on the PISA science scale and spending per student in USD converted to purchasing power parities (OECD 2007a).

In such an educational environment, the collectively accepted conception of learning extends far beyond the one that is typical to common knowledge tests. Finnish students, teachers and principals experience great degrees of autonomy and choice, but they also understand related responsibilities and expectations. I argued elsewhere that a significant proportion of the good success of Finnish schools is attributed to the fact that worthwhile learning and mutual caring about youth in schools is first, followed by responding to accountability demands in intelligent ways (Sahlberg, 2007; 2009). Although, as noted earlier, test-based accountability is not part of educational discourse in Finland, collective responsibility became more important due to systematic trust-building and cooperation endorsed by education administrations in the 1990s (Aho et al., 2006; Hargreaves et al., 2008). Specific strategies for building trust included, among other things, raising the professional status of teachers, enhancing school leadership and building professional learning communities in schools.

The main message of this chapter is that schools in market-driven education environments have been left stuck in the middle of a tough educational dilemma. The current culture of accountability in the public sector often threatens school and community social capital and damages trust, rather than supporting it. As a consequence, teachers and school leaders are no longer trusted; this decline of trust is a crisis of suspicion, as O'Neill (2002) has observed. Although the pursuit of accountability provides parents and politicians with more information, as it is employed in many places, it also builds suspicion, low morale and professional cynicism. Instead, intelligent accountability systems must be developed in order to put worthwhile learning first, and to minimize the negative effects that externally mandated, test-based accountability systems may have on teachers' work.

Today, Finland is often used as a model of successful educational change. "As societies move beyond the age of low-skill standardisation," write Hargreaves et al. (2008), "Finland contains essential lessons for nations that aspire, educationally and economically, to be successful and sustainable knowledge societies" (p. 92). However, reform ideas and policy principles that have been employed in Finland since the 1970s will not necessarily work in other cultural or social contexts. For example, Finns, like other Nordic people, exhibit higher levels of mutual trust in others and in their educational systems, when compared to people in other countries (OECD, 2008). Similarly, other socio-cultural factors come into play, as mentioned by external observers such as Grubb (2007), Hargreaves et al. (2008) and Schleicher (2006): social capital, ethnic homogeneity and high professional status of teachers. These factors may prove important when the transferability of education policies is considered.

SO WHAT?

The main message of this chapter is that schools in test-based accountability cultures and competition-driven educational environments are struggling with the expectations to teach for creativity, social justice and ecological sustainability, as I have argued elsewhere (Sahlberg, in press). Both current accountability cultures and business-like education management damage trust, rather than support it. As a consequence, teachers and school leaders are no longer trusted. The current crisis of trust in schools is a source of suspicion and fear. Although the pursuit of accountability provides parents and politicians with more information, it builds apathy, low morale and professional cynicism. Empirical evidence clearly shows that strengthening school and teacher accountability is not the best way to build sustainable knowledge societies. Alternative forms of accountability, or rather mutual responsibility and trust, is what our education systems need. One condition comes before anything else: such an accountability system must put *worthwhile learning first* and minimize the negative effects that externally mandated accountability systems may have on teachers' work.

Is more accountability in schools a way towards better quality education? After two decades of high-stakes and test-based accountability policies in England, the United States, parts of Canada and other countries, the gap between proponents and opponents in the education community is widening. The unintended consequences of high-stakes testing are becoming more evident, as presented earlier and in later chapters of this book. On the other side, accumulated testing data is used to prove that stronger school and teacher accountabilities are improving learning, closing the achievement gap and decreasing the number of early school leavers. International student assessment studies, such as the OECD PISA, also suggest that school autonomy, parental choice and accountability structures that hold schools, teachers and students accountable for determined results positively correlate with educational performance at the national level. The challenge is how to establish accountability systems that would support worthwhile learning, increase social capital and thereby help schools to be active players in developing our societies.

We are living in uncertain and insecure times. Conventional modes of schooling are becoming less and less able to provide good opportunities for learning to support sustainable societies. What we need now are more people who are able to think in new ways, work in complex situations and understand how different elements in our lives are connected. Competition is driving schools towards narrower curriculum, unified teaching and restricted creativity. At the same time, the global economic crisis, climate change and the widening gaps between rich and poor require more dynamic and responsive education systems. Schools and other educational institutions should cultivate the attitudes, cultures and skills needed in creative and collaborative learning environments.

Creativity will not flourish and be sustained in schools unless people feel secure enough to take risks and explore the unknown. Moreover, working with and understanding innovation require creative and risk-intensive learning contexts. In short, a sustainable learning society that also helps us to understand how to keep the planet's ecosystem in balance and that attempts to combat declining social capital and increasing structural indifference in many Western societies can be best promoted by developing safe and caring schools. The fear-free school is a place where students are not afraid to try new ideas and ways of thinking. Equally importantly, in the fear-free school, teachers and principals can willingly step beyond their conventional territories of thinking and doing. Often, these are conditions necessary for making substantive differences in students' learning and schools' performance. In the sustainable learning society, schools need to focus more on cultivating humanity and building social capital, rather than on becoming marketplaces where success is determined by cost-efficiency and material competition for measurable, private profit. That is our dream: genuinely caring and creative schools for all our children.

REFERENCES

Adams, R. J. (2003). Response to "Cautions on OECD's recent educational survey (PISA)". *Oxford Review of Education, 29*(3), 377–389.

Aho, E., Pitkänen, K., & Sahlberg, P. (2006). *Policy development and reform principles of basic and secondary education in Finland since 1968*. Washington, DC: World Bank.

Au, W. (2007). High-stakes testing and curricular control: A qualitative metasynthesis. *Educational Researcher, 36*(5), 258–267.

Au, W. (2008). *Unequal by design: High-stakes testing and the standardization of inequality*. London: Routledge.

Bautier, E., & Rayon, P. (2007). What PISA really evaluates: literacy or students' universes of reference? *Journal of Educational Change, 8*(4), 359–364.

Ben Jaafar, S., & Anderson, S. (2007). Policy trends and tensions in accountability for educational management and services in Canada. *Alberta Journal of Educational Research, 53*(2), 207–227.

Berry, J., & Sahlberg, P. (2006). Accountability affects the use of small group learning in school mathematics. *Nordic Studies in Mathematics Education, 11*(1), 5–31.

Carnoy, M. 1999. *Globalization and educational reform: What planners need to know?* Paris: UNESCO/IIEP.

Carnoy, M. (with A. Gove & J. Marshall). (2007). *Cuba's academic advantage: Why students in Cuba do better in school.* Stanford, CA: Stanford University Press.

Carnoy, M., & Loeb, S. (2002). Does external accountability affect student outcomes? A cross-state analysis. *Educational Evaluation and Policy Analysis, 24*(4), 305–331.

Carnoy, M., Elmore, R., & Siskin, L. (Eds.). (2003). *The new accountability. High schools and high-stakes testing.* New York: RotledgeFalmer.

Cuban, L. (2007). Hugging in the middle. Teaching in an era of testing and accountability, 1980–2005. *Education Policy Analysis Archive, 15*(1). Retrieved March 31, 2008, from http://epaa.asu.edu/epaa/v15n1/

Goldstein, H. (2004). International comparisons of student attainment: Some issues arising from the PISA study. *Assessment in Education: Principles, Policy and Practice, 11*(3), 319–330.

Grubb, N. (2007). Dynamic inequality and intervention: Lessons for a small country. *Phi Delta Kappan, 89*(2), 105–114.

Hamilton, L., Stecher, B., & Klein, S. (Eds.). (2002). *Making sense of test-based account-ability in education.* Santa Monica: RAND.

Hargreaves, A. (2003). *Teaching in the knowledge society: Education in the age of insecurity.* New York: Teachers College Press.

Hargreaves, A. (2008). The fourth way of change: Towards an age of inspiration and sustainability. In A. Hargreaves & M. Fullan (Eds.), *Change wars.* Toronto: Solution Tree.

Hargreaves, A., & Fink, D. (2005). *Sustainable leadership.* San Francisco: Jossey-Bass.

Hargreaves, A., & Goodson, I. (2006). Educational change over time? The sustainability and nonsustainability of three decades of secondary school change and continuity. *Educational Administration Quarterly, 42*(1), 3–41.

Hargreaves, A., & Shirley, D. (in press). The fourth way: The inspiring future for educational change. Thousand Oaks, CA: Corwin Press.

Hargreaves, A., Halasz, G., & Pont, B. (2008). The Finnish approach to system leadership. In B. Pont, D. Nusche, & D. Hopkins (Eds.), *Improving school leadership, Volume 2: Case studies on system leadership* (pp. 69–109). Paris: OECD.

Itkonen, T., & Jahnukainen, M. (2007). An analysis of accountability policies in Finland and the United States. *International Journal of Disability, Development and Education, 54*(1), 5–23.

Jones, M., Jones, B., & Hargrove, T. (2003). *The unintended consequences of high-stakes testing.* Lanham, MD: Rowman & Littlefield.

Kupari, P., & Välijärvi, J. (Eds.). (2005). Osaaminen kestävällä pohjalla: PISA 2003 Suomessa [Competencies on solid ground: PISA 2003 in Finland]. Jyväskylä: Institute for Educational Research, University of Jyväskylä.

Ladd, H., & Fiske, E. (2003). Does competition improve teaching and learning? Evidence from New Zealand. *Educational Evaluation and Policy Analysis, 25*(1), 97–112.

Laukkanen, R. (1998). Accountability and evaluation: Decision-making structures and the utilization of evaluation in Finland. *Scandinavian Journal of Educational Research, 42*(2), 123–133.

Laukkanen, R. (2008). Finnish strategy for high-level education for all. In N.C. Soguel & P. Jaccard (Eds.), *Governance and Performance of Education Systems* (pp. 305–324). New York: Springer.

Levin, B. (2001). *Reforming education: From origins to outcomes.* London: Routledge Falmer.

Levin, B., & Fullan, M. (2008). Learning about system renewal. *Educational Management, Administration and Leadership, 36*(2), 289–303.

Loeb, H., Knapp, M., & Elfers, A. (2008). Teachers' response to standards-based reform: Probing reform assumptions in Washington State. *Education Policy Analysis Archives, 16*(9). Retrieved May 1, 2008, from http://epaa.asu.edu/epaa/v16n9/

Lortie, D. (1975). *Schoolteacher: A sociological study*. Chicago: University of Chicago Press.

McNeil, L. (2000). *Contradictions of school reform: Educational costs of standardized testing*. New York: Routledge.

McNeil, L., Coppola, E., Radigan, J., & Vasquez Heilig, J. (2008). Avoidable losses: High-stakes accountability and the dropout crisis. *Education Policy Analysis Archives, 16*(3). Retrieved May 1, 2008, from http://epaa.asu.edu/epaa/v16n3/

Nagy, P. (1996). International comparisons of student achievement in mathematics and science: A Canadian perspective. *Canadian Journal of Education, 21*(4), 396–413.

Nichols, S., & Berliner, D. (2007). *Collateral damage: How high-stakes testing corrupts America's schools*. Cambridge, MA: Harvard Education Press.

O'Neill, O. (2002). *A question of trust*. Cambridge: Cambridge University Press.

OECD. (2001). *Knowledge and skills for life: First results from PISA 2000*. Paris: Author.

OECD. (2004). *Learning for tomorrow's world. First results from PISA 2003*. Paris: Author.

OECD. (2007a). *PISA 2006: Science competencies for tomorrow's world* (Vol. 1). Paris: Author.

OECD. (2007b). *Education at a glance: OECD indicators 2007*. Paris: Author.

OECD. (2008). *Trends shaping education*. Paris: Author.

Popham, J. (2007). The no-win accountability game. In C. Glickman (Ed.), *Letters to the next President: What we can do about the real crisis in public education* (pp. 166–173). New York: Teachers College Press.

Prais, S. J. (2003). Cautions on OECD's recent educational survey (PISA). *Oxford Review of Education, 29*(2), 139–163.

Prais, S. J. (2004). Cautions on OECD's recent educational survey (PISA): Rejoinder to OECD's response. *Oxford Review of Education, 30*(4), 569–573.

Rees, M. (2003). *Our final century: A scientist's warning: How terror, error, and environmental disaster threaten humankind's future in this century, on Earth and beyond*. London: Heinemann.

Riley, K., & Torrance, H. (2003). Big change question: As national policy-makers seek to find solutions to national education issues, do international comparisons such as TIMSS and PISA create a wider understanding, or do they serve to promote the orthodoxies of international agencies? *Journal of Educational Change, 4*(4), 419–425.

Robitaille, D. F., & Garden, R. A. (Eds.). (1989). *The IEA study of mathematics II: Context and outcomes of school mathematics*. Oxford: Pergamon Press.

Sachs, J. (2008). *Common wealth. Economics for a crowded planet*. New York: Penguin.

Sacks, P. (2001). *Standardized minds: The high price of America's testing culture and what we can do to change it*. New York: Perseus.

Sahlberg, P. (2006). Education reform for raising economic competitiveness. *Journal of Educational Change, 7*(4), 259–287.

Sahlberg, P. (2007). Education policies for raising student learning: The Finnish approach. *Journal of Education Policy, 22*(2), 147–171.

Sahlberg, P. (2009). Educational change in Finland. In A. Hargreaves, M. Fullan, A. Lieberman, & D. Hopkins (Eds.), *International handbook of educational change* (2nd ed.). New York: Kluwer.

Sahlberg, P. (in press). Rethinking accountability in a knowledge society. *Journal of Educational Change*.

Schleicher, A. (2006). *The economics of knowledge: Why education is key for Europe's success*. Brussels: Lisbon Council.

Secondary School Heads Association. (2003). *Towards intelligent accountability for schools: A policy statement on school accountability*. Leicester: Secondary Heads Association.

Sharan, S., & Chin Tan, I. (2008). *Organizing schools for productive learning*. New York: Springer.

Shirley, D. (2008, March 28). *All communities left behind? How new school accountability and performance regimes undermine sustainable civic capacity in recent US reforms*. Paper presented at AERA annual meeting, New York, NY.

Statistics Finland. (2007). *Education*. Retrieved December 30, 2007, from http://www.stat.fi/til/kou_en.html

Teacher suspended for refusing to give state test. (2008, April). *Teacher magazine*. Retrieved April 22, 2008, from http://www.teachermagazine.org/tm/articles/2008/04/22/notest_ap.h19.html

Tschannen-Moran, M. (2007). Becoming a trustworthy leader. In *The Jossey-Bass reader on educational leadership* (pp. 99–113). San Francisco: John Wiley and Sons, Inc.

Wössmann, L., Lüdemann, E., Schütz, G., & West, M. (2007). *School accountability, autonomy and choice, and the level of student achievement: International evidence from PISA 2003*. Paris: OECD.

SHELLEY WILLIER

2. ACCOUNTABILITY IN FIRST NATIONS EDUCATION

Kwāyāsk Etōtamihk (Doing it Right)[i]

OSKAC (INTRODUCTION)

Almost a decade ago, Waite, Boone, and McGhee (2001) found that the term *accountability* "so deeply...infiltrated public dialogue [in education] that its meanings, connotations, and ramifications remain largely unquestioned" (p. 183). Because educational accountability has come to shape public schooling, it is important that caution is exercised when critiquing accountability initiatives, since "accountability" is often value-laden and can be understood in various ways. As Waite et al. point out, "when people write or speak of accountability...the meaning is often ambiguous...and there is no consensus regarding all the variables that should/would constitute [the term's concepts or domains]" (p. 183). Since there have always been competing narratives about what education is and how it ought to be delivered to First Nations people, it stands to reason that the values related to the idea of accountability will be controversial as well.

In this chapter, I present an historical overview of First Nations education to provide the background necessary for understanding my critique of current accountability policies as they relate to First Nations schools and communities in Alberta. Next, using Alberta's new First Nations, Métis and Inuit (FNMI) and *accountability pillar* policies as an example, I point out the contradiction that often exist in initiatives that are meant to serve First Nations students. I also discuss the tensions that are inherent in the federal, provincial, and First Nations involvement in educational provision, using accountability as an example of how unique and often conflicting positions continue to undermine First Nations education. I then argue that the Cree ideas of responsibility, relationship and community could be used to develop an understanding that provides an alternative to current conceptions of accountability and that is more appropriate for transforming public education to meet the needs and goals of First Nations people.

PIMOHTEWIN (THE JOURNEY): TRADITIONAL TO CONTEMPORARY FIRST NATIONS EDUCATION

First Nations epistemology (i.e., ways of knowing) has been maintained from generation to generation through structures of language (Battiste, 1998), modeling, practice and experience. When asked for his understanding of traditional Aboriginal education, a Sucker Creek First Nation Elder shared:

K.D. Gariepy, B.L. Spencer and J.-C. Couture (eds.), Educational Accountability:
Professional Voices From the Field, 23–34.
© 2009 Sense Publishers. All rights reserved.

Indian education was geared for survival. We hunted moose to live. We ate the meat and used the hide to keep us warm. The family worked together to live and learn. The family was the center of everything. The adults passed knowledge through language on to the kids so they would live. They also showed the kids what to do by doing. (P. Willier, personal communication, July, 2005)

This Elder's narrative reveals that traditional education centered on the child and that everyone lived the ideal of *miyo-wîcîhtôwin*, (helping each other in a good way). Language was imperative in the process of expressing meaning, value, and culture. Our *nehiyaw-itâpisiniwin*, or Cree place of sight (viewpoint), was shared through the way we were and the way we spoke.

A review of the research about traditional Aboriginal education reflects the sentiments above and identifies the following values:
- Through Indian tradition each adult was personally responsible for each child, to see that he learned all he needed to know in order to live a good life (National Indian Brotherhood [NIB], 1973).
- Each person was responsible for keeping the self (mind, body, spirit, emotion) healthy. To achieve that goal, the self interacted with the family, these interacted with the community, and these three spheres interacted with society (Assembly of First Nations Language and Literacy Secretariat, 1994).
- "Indigenous pedagogical principles were holistic, connected, valid, culturally-based, value-based, thematic and experiential. They promoted and rewarded cooperative learning and the unified co-operation of learners and teachers. Indigenous pedagogical principles, unlike Western paradigms, recognized the important role of non-verbal communication in the learning-teaching process" ("Coolangatta Statement on Indigenous Peoples' Rights in Education," 1999).

Traditional Aboriginal education focuses on knowledge that is shared through language and culture, and relationships are a natural and integral part of teaching and learning. Learners are related to their teachers and teachers to their learners– the circle is complete. Nothing is learned in isolation.

In Canada, treaties between First Nations and the federal government changed the face of education for First Nations people. When Treaty No. 8 was signed in 1899, for example, several promises were made to First Nations people, one being the right to a "new" form of education. The vision of our Elders at the signing of the Treaty was to enable member First Nations to be enriched by a new knowledge system that would *supplement* traditional knowledge (Henderson, 1995). Unfortunately, this vision never came to fruition. Under the authority of the Indian Act, the Crown, presuming to have superior knowledge, chose to impose an education system that exalted Western knowledge, attitudes, skills and values over those of First Nations people. By dismissing the importance of First Nations traditions, knowledge, culture, language and lifestyles and by denying First Nations people access to their traditional education system, the Crown effectively established a system of education which oppressed and exploited First Nations people. A process of assimilation and cultural genocide began with the explicit goal of "Kill the Indian, save the child" (Thompson, 2001). As one Cree elder reflects,

The government decided to assimilate Indians at the time of residential schools. They educated by taking away. The older people thought that school was good because they were brainwashed by the priests into believing their kids were being cared for. They didn't see the abuse. They didn't see the priests steal our language and culture...they robbed us of who we were. They tried to beat the language out of us. We used to get strapped on our upper arms because it was tenderer there. We all had deep purple welts...a sign that we did something very wrong. (P. Willier, personal communication, July, 2005)

This experience of guilt and shame left a legacy of broken spirits and suppression of identity, but the task of assimilating First Nations people did not stop at robbing children of their language, culture, and identity. When one culture dominates another that is perceived as inferior, the control of education and its delivery is imperative to establishing and maintaining power through limiting educational opportunities, which are directly linked to livelihood and economic status. In First Nations education, curriculum focused only on those basic skills deemed relevant to the Indian who would return to the reservation (Hutchings, n.d.). This education was not to be questioned, interpreted, or reflected upon by the learner and was based upon a foreign value system. As Bolotin (2000) points out, this approach works as a hidden curriculum, a kind of socialization that covertly shapes the morals and values of those being taught.

MEKWĀC KĀ ISPAYIK (THE WAY IT IS): CURRICULUM AND PROGRAMMES, GOVERNANCE AND FUNDING IN FIRST NATIONS EDUCATION

Although there have been initiatives to address the dominant, Western assumptions of education and the resulting oppression and inequity[i], the urgent need for improving educational opportunities and completion rates for First Nations continues to be paramount. If schools are indeed to be a reflection of society, then the philosophy of fairness and equity that Canada embraces should be reflected in the funding, principles, policies, and guidelines that govern First Nations schools. Presently, this is sorely lacking. One example in response to this situation is Alberta Learning's (2002) FNMI. Promising practices have resulted from this framework and data collected through two case studies reveal Aboriginal learner success (Alberta Education, 2008b). However, although FNMI programming demonstrates Alberta Education's leadership in First Nations education, it should be noted that many of the province's First Nations students do not benefit from the FNMI initiatives because they attend band-operated schools outside of Alberta Education's jurisdiction. Moreover, while the framework has brought attention to First Nations issues and has introduced FNMI perspectives, curriculum, programming and approaches, these new initiatives are ultimately subject to Alberta's overall accountability framework. This framework remains rooted in dominant, Western notions about assessment and student achievement and includes *accountability pillar* policies (e.g., large-scale standardized testing and outcomes-based reporting) that mandate results that are measurable and comparable in terms of province-wide standards (Alberta Education, 2008a).

Here it must be noted that, by the standards stipulated by the *accountability pillar*, aggregate results show that Alberta's First Nations schools do not do well, even while the policies and strategies are meant to close the gap between standards and achievement. Research that has investigated other such accountability frameworks (e.g., the *No Child Left Behind* policies in the U.S.) and their success in "closing the gap" for minority students provides important insights. For example, the assumptions and contradictions inherent in the attempts to remedy the "problem" of under-achieving students by imposing standards that focus attention on educational *outcomes* rather than on *process* can actually be detrimental to those whose interests the policies are meant to serve (Scheurich, Skrla, & Johnson, 2004; Waite et al., 2001). Specifically, lessons about culturally biased tests, the problems of "one size fits all" standards and the unintended effects of large-scale testing (e.g., "teaching to the test" and students who choose to drop out rather than fail) should be heeded before claims are made that Alberta's accountability framework serves *all* of Alberta's students. This could be the subject of a review. As the Alberta Teachers' Association (2005) points out, since its implementation, the *accountability pillar* itself has never been through a process of assessment and evaluation.

In addition to the accountability contradictions related to curriculum and programming are contradictions related to funding and governance. In 1973, the NIB authored the ground-breaking paper *Indian Control of Indian Education*. The NIB's primary recommendation was the decentralization of First Nations education, which it argued would provide "opportunities for local people to have a say in school governance, [restoring] to them the feeling that they are not powerless, and that they are in control of their destinies" (Agbo, 2002, p. 283). The federal government's response to the paper was that Indian and Northern Affairs Canada (INAC) would continue its funding of education for First Nations students and would support the creation of band-operated schools. This inter-agency involvement contributed to disorder and misunderstanding. This situation, as Brady (1995) argues, "leaves Native governments in the unenviable position of being responsible for delivering a variety of services without having complete control over many parameters directly affecting delivery..." (p. 357). As Wilson (2007) suggests, the jurisdictional complexity related to federal, provincial and band involvement in First Nations schools has resulted in a "gray zone" where power struggles keep First Nations mired in the political language of self-governance, sovereignty, accountability and cultural survival (p. 248). An example of this "gray zone" as it relates to accountability is as follows.

First, accountability measures for First Nations education at the federal level are linked to the transfer of education dollars from the federal government to First Nations authorities via funding transfers set up by INAC. Carr-Stewart (2006) found that INAC's funding supports the maintenance of minimum levels of education provision. Second, at the same time, band-operated schools are obligated to complete a "School Declaration of Program" process, an accountability measure designed to "ensure [that] Band-operated Schools [comply] with government requirements" (Alberta Education Budget and Fiscal Analysis Branch, 2008). Third, band-operated schools, like public schools, must also adhere to Alberta Education's *accountability pillar*, which "provides a ... way for school authorities to measure success, assess their progress and share results (Alberta Education, 2008a). In reality, these three accountability measures, which conflict, do not help ensure that First Nations students are provided with the high quality education desired for *all* Albertans. This reinforces the historical inequities that have plagued First Nations people.

As suggested by this example, without true devolution of power through self-governance, First Nations communities do not have authority to make informed decisions and to "get things done," let alone address the inequities that are the effects of a contentious accountability context. As Agbo (2002) points out, "few would deny that First Nations schools should be accountable. However, this is an empty assertion unless we also state clearly the form, extent, and character of their accountability" (p. 294). If the ideal of First Nations self-governance were upheld, First Nations *themselves* would possess the power to develop their *own* processes of determining goals, assessing achievement and defining student success. They would develop their *own* accountability framework.

EWĪ-AYIMAHK (IT'S GOING TO BE DIFFICULT): CHALLENGING THE CONCEPT OF ACCOUNTABILITY

Leithwood and Earl (2000) offer the following questions to assist in understanding accountability: *What level of accountability is to be provided? Who is expected to provide this account? To whom is the account owed? What is to be accounted for? What are the consequences of providing the account?* (p. 2). These questions can be helpful in providing direction for developing accountability policies. However, from a First Nations perspective, they centre on ontological and epistemological notions that are, in the first place, Eurocentric. In addition, in current contexts, such as Alberta, they have come to take on definitions of accountability that are highly influenced by neoliberal assumptions about standards, quality, efficiency, effectiveness and the importance of competition in a market economy (Ben Jaafar & Anderson, 2007)–values that are not held by all. What these questions lack is sufficient attention to *whose* conceptions of accountability are privileged. The consideration of *who* potentially creates space for understanding that accountability is not a universal, neutral concept.

OTE NĪKĀN (IN THE FUTURE): LOOKING AT THEORY IN EDUCATIONAL CHANGE

It may be helpful to examine current thinking about educational change when considering the future of First Nations education and the accountability policies and practices that might shape it. For example, Hargreaves (2009) advocates for a change-in-action theory that focuses on shared partnerships with a "bold and inclusive vision that unites and energizes people" (An Inspiring and Inclusive Vision section, para. 1). He argues for education systems that rely on trust and relationship building, characterized by "a compelling and inclusive moral purpose steer[ing] [the] system, bind[ing] it together and draw[ing] the best people to work in it" (An Inspiring and Inclusive Vision section, para. 4). Discussions surrounding transformation in First Nations education can draw upon Hargreaves's idea that "...accountability is the remainder that is left when responsibility has been subtracted..." (Responsibility Before Accountability section, para. 1). This resonates with traditional First Nations cultural values and practices. For example, because roles are clearly defined in First Nations communities, if I, as a First Nations woman, take on my roles of daughter, mother, sister, aunt, friend, teacher and learner, and "do right" by them, I will naturally perform these roles with responsibility because responsibility is inextricably linked to relationships in my community.

Brendtro, Brokenleg, and Van Bockern's (2002) discuss the importance of relationships in their "Circle of Courage," which consists of the following ideals: belonging, mastery, independence, and generosity. Paramount among these is belonging, because being valued, welcomed, and comforted within a group of family, friends, and community is fundamental to human development (pp. 43-57). The Cree belief that every child has many mothers (P. Willier, personal communication, July 2005), epitomizes this ideal. In First Nations communities, treating each other as though we are relatives is a "core social value that transform[s] relationships. Drawing [others] into one's circle motivate[s] one to show respect and concern, and [to] live with a minimum of friction and a maximum of good will" (p. 47). *Kwayask nīma wīkowāhk ohpikihitowak,* or feeling like you belong, is the basis of being.

AWINA MĀKA KIYA (WHO IS IT THAT YOU REALLY ARE?): IDENTITY IN EDUCATION

When thinking about roles, responsibilities and establishing a sense of belonging in First Nations education, we must see identity as central because it holds our ways of knowing and seeing the world. Identity is also key in establishing laws, principles, and guidelines which lead to doing what is right for our people. In 2005, I conducted a very informal interview with my father, meant to inquire about the state of change in First Nations education. One specific question I asked him was: *Is identity important to education?* I did not receive a yes or no answer; what I received was an answer embedded in the following oration:

Identity. What is identity? Do you actually think you can find it? That is the biggest excuse I ever heard: "I'm going to find myself, I don't know who I am." It's an excuse...to be lazy. We knew who we were long ago. Peter was born Peter. My mother, my father, my sisters and brothers...they all knew who Peter was.

Peter became Peter because of my family. I didn't have to go find him. I knew who he was when I went to school and when I went to work because he is, was me. You guys ignore who you are, not because you don't know, but because knowing is too hard. That is what the world has done to you. It has made you lazy. (P. Willier, personal communication, July 2005)

My father holds the belief that a person is born with an identity already intact. Identity is inherent, not something that is created or taken away. This statement might appear to be contrary to what my father said when he spoke, "Peter became Peter because of my family," but it is not. Peter did not become Peter because his family created him; rather, he became Peter through the relationships he had with them, the values they instilled in him and the language and culture that surrounded him. His family provided a support system that unearthed what was already there. They provided an environment conducive for Peter to be.

My father expressed words of wisdom. The message is simple: you cannot go outside yourself to find yourself because you are already there. Unearthing knowledge about your self is a continuous, never-ending process that leads to an ever-increasing understanding as you grow with time, age, experience, and relationships. It is the process of seeking and living truth. In order for truth to "be," you must live it. Once truth becomes lived, you are walking in an honest manner. This is a difficult task and is what my father referred to when he spoke of being "lazy." The importance of walking in an honest manner is why he warns against denying truth, letting externals persuade us that we do not know who we are and taking on a foreign identity. This is a lesson of the history of First Nations education, especially in light of the legacy of residential schools.

One's identity is also related to methods of learning. As Cardinal (2005) explains, First Nations people are of four worlds, and these inherent worlds connect us as family, community, people, learners and teachers:

> Many years ago a Cree Elder asked me a question: Awina maga kiya- who is it that you really are? I replied in Cree – Neehiyow neyah – at that time, I thought I was saying "I am Indian." The Cree Elder then asked in Cree: Ta ni ki maga "Nee hiyow" Kee tig a wee yin? Tansi ee twee maga? Why is it that you are called "Neehiyow"- what does the word mean? When the Elder realized that I did not fully understand the meaning of the word, the Elder proceeded to explain.

> The word "Ni hi yow" comes from two words in our language: 1) Neewoo-four and 2) Yow-body [world]. In the context in which I use the term, it means: Four bodies...we believe that knowledge [is placed] in each of the four worlds. When we say that "I am a Ni Hi Yow" what I am really saying is that I come from "the people who seek the knowledge of the four worlds." In short when I apply the word "Ni Hi Yow" to myself, what I am saying is that "I am a seeker of knowledge."

Cardinal acknowledges that Indigenous people seek knowledge of all things, including identity (self), but it was through the Elder that he came to understand the full truth of who he really is: that of four worlds. These worlds (i.e., ways of knowing), are mind, body, spirit, and emotion. This is the holistic concept of self.

The stories of my father and the Cree Elder are very powerful. Both men state that learning first comes from within one's self and that this learning is enhanced through relationships with others. Relationship building should therefore be of the utmost importance in contemporary schools, since "schooling is more than a set of technical or organizational arrangements. It is also an interpersonal and moral enterprise, because it involves social relationships and seeks to regulate and [enhance] character or personality" (Schissel & Wotherspoon, 2003, p. 31). In First Nations education, character and personality are understood as identity, and the enhancement of identify must be based on Indigenous natural laws. Makokis (as cited in Steinhauer, 2002) describes the laws this way:

- Love/Kindness-Kiseywatisowin, which basically tells us that before we can be humble, we have to be kind, and that we must feel with our heart, not just our mind.
- Honesty-Kweyaskatesown. Kwesask is the root word and refers to being aligned and straight. Itatisowin is the verb and implies characteristics or a trait of being in life. We are to lead honest lives. For whatever we do, we must do it in complete honesty with ourselves and others. This keeps our heart, mind, and spirit full of integrity.
- Sharing-Wichihtowin. This word stems from wichih, to help, towin makes the root work into a noun and refers to having everybody involved.
- Strength-Sohkisowin. This word refers to strength and determination in the body, and sohkeyihtamowin is the strength. (p. 79)

Living by these natural laws is our way of "thinking right," which is necessary before we can "do right." "Doing right" means acting in an ethical and responsible manner. Who I am (my identity) determines how I act. Western understandings of education are not devoid of some of these ideas. For example, Starratt's (2004) research into responsibility reveals that "in a given role, one will perform as a morally responsible agent" (p. 47). Following this, decisions made in education would not be arbitrary but could take "due deliberation on circumstances and the values that apply to the situation as well as caring for the persons who will be affected by the decision" (p. 47). Specific to educational leadership, Starratt argues that educational leaders must have knowledge of who they are as leaders and what they are responsible for. He advocates that once a "right way of thinking" about identity and responsibility has been established, a "right way of doing" things will emerge and will potentially lead to new understandings of accountability.

SŌHKISOWIN (IT IS POWERFUL): RE-FRAMING ACCOUNTABILITY

When discussing accountability from a First Nations Cree point of view, difficulty arises in the fact that there is no direct translation for "accountability" within our language structure (F. Badger, Personal Communication, August, 2008). As discussed above, our tongue speaks of roles, responsibilities and doing things right: *kwāyāsk etōtamihk*. Therefore, from a Cree perspective, it is responsibility, not accountability, that ensures that we "do the right thing." The concept of *kwāyāsk etōtamihk* works within the principles of *wāhkōhtowin* (a coming together of people; a state of relationship building) and *wicihtowin* (the sharing of everything and everyone). Working within these concepts in K-12 First Nations education would help render current accountability policies and practices unnecessary. Through *māmawi wīhkōhtowin ekwa māmawimōwin* (pulling together and sharing), the Elders' vision at the signing of our treaties, of a new knowledge system complimenting traditional knowledge, could be realized. These principles and ideals could also allow First Nations leaders to establish a culture of belonging in their schools and educational systems, since First Nations ontology and epistemology would be the foundation of knowledge creation and program delivery. When examining the concept of responsibility in First Nations education (i.e., relationships and belonging, identity and thinking and doing right), it is important to remember that:

Aboriginal philosophies of education were based on the assumptions that

education is life-long and that teaching should prepare young people to participate fully in the spiritual, cultural, physical, and emotional life of the society. In an educational context like this, the concepts of "failure" and "pass" are irrelevant. (Schissel & Wotherspoon, 2003, p. 63)

With these beliefs in mind, First Nations education must focus on more than high standards and competition, which seem to permeate mainstream understandings of educational accountability. More emphasis needs to be placed on the concepts of *nihiyaw* and *pimacihowin*, which stress the importance of seeking knowledge within four worlds and making a living. In this way, First Nations education might better provide our people with the knowledge, skills and attitudes needed to improve their quality of life.

MĀCIKA OMISI KĀ KĪ ISPAYIK (SUMMATION)

Although education should be a means of fulfilling hopes and dreams, for First Nations it has often been a way of keeping a group of people in a state of continuous disadvantage. The issue of transforming First Nations education is a pressing problem. Attempting to incorporate First Nations values while struggling with accountability contradictions, jurisdictional tensions and political inertia and the differences in the language and meaning of accountability is the challenge that we face. In order for educational partners to work together to improve education for First Nations people, educational policies and practices must reflect the values of all participants. In order for First Nations people to walk successfully in both worlds, guidance needs to come from the best of traditional First Nations education. Educational leaders must also model the willingness to do what is right for First Nations students. By placing learners first and centering the values of responsibility and relationships, a right way of thinking may be established, and issues in First Nations education concerning appropriate curriculum and programming and funding and governance could be better addressed, since the focus would be on the "right thing to do."

In conclusion, I would like to foreground the following Cree teachings as possible ways to focus on responsibility and to guide alternative understandings of educational accountability in First Nations education.

Kwayask Māmawi Wīhkōhtowin Ekwa Māmawimōwin (the process of pulling together and sharing in a right way): In regards to relationship building, positive and relevant family and community engagement in the education process of First Nations learners is essential for enhancing First Nations identity and establishing a sense of belonging.

Kwayask Nīma Wīkowāhk Ohpikihitowak (the process of establishing a sense of belonging): Establishing a "sense of belonging" in schools and school systems is the basis of a positive school culture. A positive school culture for First Nations learners is one that instills pride in being First Nations and instills confidence to be a successful life-long learner.

Nitokiskisiwin (the process of reflecting on how actions, thoughts and feelings impact ourselves and others): Reflection is a way of determining whether roles and responsibilities within a system are being met and a way of determining what changes, if any, are needed to support teaching and learning.

Awina Māka Kiya (the process of showing who you really are): It is important that First Nations educators answer the following questions in personal growth plans: *Who am I as a professional in First Nations education? What is my role? What responsibilities are associated with my current role? What responsibilities do I perform well? What responsibilities are my areas of focus?* As plans are reviewed, an approach to educational development that benefits both teacher and learner can be taken.

Kwayask Kiskinohamākewin (or excellence in education): Because teacher-learner relationships are symbiotic, it follows that the best of our teachers bring out the best in our students. Excellent teachers do not support learners alone. They work collegially with peers, family, and community, and they employ a variety of pedagogical strategies to enhance learner strengths and meet their needs.

Kwayask Enīkānapit (or quality leadership in education): Educational leadership is a relationship that exists between leader, teacher and learner wherein knowledge, skills and attitudes are shared and acquired by all. Leadership affects the delivery of programming in the school, the sharing of knowledge in the classroom and the environment in which teaching and learning take place.

Kīkway Kā Kakwe Kiskiyihtaman (the processes of trying to know, gathering knowledge and answering the question *What are you trying to learn?*): Acknowledging students' unique positions and experiences, their sense of identity and their specific learning goals.

Kwayask Ōma Kā Ispayik (the process of honouring what is right): Schools would celebrate language and culture, Elder leadership, traditional character development (respect, love/kindness, honour, humility, truth/honesty, courage, and wisdom) and relationships (parent/community engagement) in ways that would compliment academics.

Ote Nīkān (the process of looking ahead into the future): This allows First Nations to determine the direction they are moving in, what their relationships will be within the global society and the responsibilities they will have in the future.

NOTES

[1] Thanks to Peter Willier, Georgina Willier, Sally Badger and Fred Badger for assistance with Cree words and definitions and Billy Joe Laboucan for assistance with Cree spelling and diacritics.
[2] For a discussion about some of these initiatives, see Carr-Stewart (2006) on Citizens Plus (1970), the National Indian Brotherhood (1973), INAC (2008) and chapter 5 of the November 2004 report of the Office of the Auditor General.

REFERENCES

Agbo, S. A. (2002). Decentralization of First Nations education in Canada: Perspectives on ideals and realities of Indian control of Indian education. *Interchange, 33*(3), 281–302.

Alberta Education. (2008a). *Accountability in Alberta's education system.* Retrieved January 30, 2009, from http://education.alberta.ca/admin/funding/accountability.aspx

Alberta Education. (2008b). *Promising practices in First Nations, Mets and Inuit education.* Retrieved January 30, 2009, from http://education.alberta.ca/media/859897/promising%20practices%20case %20 studies %20two.pdf

Alberta Education Budget and Fiscal Analysis Branch. (2008). *The renewed funding framework: Education funding for Alberta school jurisdictions: 2008/2009 School Year.* Retrieved January 30, 2009, http://www.assembly.ab.ca/lao/library/egovdocs/2008/aled/168709.pdf

Alberta Learning. (2002). *First Nations, Métis and Inuit education policy framework.* Retrieved January 30, 2009, from http://www.education.alberta.ca/teachers/fnmi/fnmipolicy.aspx

Alberta Teachers' Association. (2005). *Accountability in education: Background paper.* Retrieved February 2, 2009, from http://www.teachers.ab.ca/SiteCollectionDocuments/ATA/Issues%20In%20 Education/Emerging%20Issues/Accountability%20Discussion%20Paper.pdf

Assembly of First Nations Language and Literacy Secretariat. (1994). *Breaking the chains: First Nations literacy and self-determination.* Ottawa: Assembly of First Nations.

Battiste, M. (1998). Enabling the autumn seed: Toward a decolonized approach to Aboriginal knowledge, language, and education. *Canadian Journal of Native Education, 22*(1), 16–27.

Ben Jaafar, S., & Anderson, S. (2007). Policy trends and tensions in accountability for educational management and services in Canada. *Alberta Journal of Educational Research, 53*(2), 207–221.

Bolotin, J. P. (2000). Conceptualizing curriculum. In P. B. Joseph, S. L. Bravmann, M. A., Windschitl, E. R. Mikel, & N. S. Green (Eds.), *Cultures of curriculum* (pp. 1–14). Mahwah, NJ: L. Erlbaum Associates.

Brady, P. (1995). Two policy approaches to Native education: Can reform be legislated? *Canadian Journal of Educational Administration and Policy, 20*(3), 281–302.

Brendtro, L., Brokenleg, M., & Van Bockern, S. (2002). *Reclaiming youth at risk: Our hope for the future.* Bloomington, IN: National Educational Service.

Cardinal, H. (2005). *Einew lis-kee-tum-awin: Indigenous People's knowledge.* Paper presented at the Treaty 8 First Nations of Alberta Scholar's Think Tank #2, Edmonton, AB.

Carr-Stewart, S. (2006). First Nations education: Financial accountability and educational attainment. *Canadian Journal of Educational Administration and Policy, 29*(4), 998–1018.

Coolangatta statement on Indigenous Peoples' rights in education. (1999). Retrieved January 30, 2009, from http://www.ankn.uaf.edu/IKS/cool.html

Hargreaves, A. (2009). The fourth way of change: Towards an age of inspiration and sustainablity. In A. Hargreaves & M. Fullan (Eds.), *Change wars.* Bloomington, IN: Solution Tree.

Henderson, J. Y. (1995). *Indian education and treaties.* In M. Battiste & J. Barman (Eds.), *First Nations education in Canada: The circle unfolds.* Vancouver: University of British Columbia.

Hutchings, C. (n.d.). *Canada's First Nations: A legacy of institutional racism.* Retrieved June 12, 2005, from http://www.tolerance.cz/courses/papers/hutchin.htm

Leithwood, K., & Earl, L. (2000). Educational accountability effects: An international perspective. *Peabody Journal of Education, 75*(4), 1–18.

National Indian Brotherhood. (1973). *Indian control of Indian education.* Ottawa: National Indian Brotherhood.

Office of the Auditor General of Canada. (2004). *Chapter 5: Indian and Northern Affairs Canada: Education program and post secondary student support.* Retrieved January 30, 2009, from http://www.oag-bvg.gc.ca/internet/English/parl_oag_200411_05_e_14909.html

Schissel, B., & Wotherspoon, T. (2003). *The legacy of school for Aboriginal people: Education, oppression and emancipation.* Don Mills, ON: Oxford University Press.

Scheurich, J. J., Skrla, L., & Johnston, J. F., Jr. (2004). Thinking carefully about equity and accountability. In L. Skrla & J. J. Scheurich (Eds.), *Educational equity and accountability: Paradigms, policies, and politics* (pp. 13–27). New York: RoutledgeFalmer.

Starratt, R. (2004). *Ethical leadership.* San Francisco: Jossey-Bass.

Steinhauer, E. (2002). Thoughts on an Indigenous research methodology. *Canadian Journal of Native Education, 26*(2), 69–80.

Thompson, M. (2001). *Charles Lummis: Indian rights crusader.* Retrieved May 10, 2008, from http://www.charleslummis.com/indianrights.htm

Waite, D., Boone, M., & McGhee, M. (2001). A critical sociocultural view of accountability. *Journal of School Leadership, 11*(3), 182–203.

Wilson, J. B., (2007). First Nations education: The need for legislation in the jurisdictional gray zone. *Canadian Journal of Native Education, 301*(2), 248–256.

TROY DAVIES

3. SCHOOL CHOICE AND ACCOUNTABILITY IN ALBERTA

Similar to the experience of all other school principals in Alberta, my workaday world finds me mired in a seemingly endless array of tasks. The work is challenging, consuming and often unfolds at a frenzied pace. Given the unrelenting busyness, it can be extremely difficult for those like me, in leadership roles, to carve out occasions when it is possible to gain perspective on the policy contexts within which we perform our professional roles. Thankfully, I have been afforded this opportunity. For the past 3 years I have been studying as a doctoral student in the area of educational administration and leadership. This experience has given me the chance to explore matters from a different, broader vantage point than is the case when I am fully hunkered down in the trenches of my school site. Heifetz and Linsky (2002) call this "'getting off the dance floor and going to the balcony', an image that captures the mental activity of stepping back in the midst of action and asking, 'What's really going on here?'" (p. 51).

From the balcony, I perceive that there has been a shift in Alberta in recent years with regard to school choice, especially as it now relates to accountability. I find myself wondering about how these two policy issues work together. Specifically, I am curious about how some of the choice programs that have existed for many years in Alberta operate, considering they now exist within a larger system where accountability policies have become increasingly encompassing. My current reading of the literature and research related to school choice and accountability is challenging me to think about the ways in which these policy concerns function not as disparate entities but, rather, in tandem to create quasi-market conditions for public education provision. Here, my interest is in the possible effects of the school choice-accountability combination that is still a fairly recent reality in Alberta. Thus, this chapter is not intended to be a critique of Alberta's school choice programs, nor is it a complaint about accountability policies; rather, it is my attempt to lend some analysis to these issues in an effort to understand them better.

In this chapter I endeavour to answer the following questions: Where do these ideas and policies about school choice and accountability originate? What are the links and associations between the two? What are the effects of these connections? How do schools respond to the quasi-market conditions that these connections may engender? In addressing these questions, I rely on what the literature says about both the extra-local context, which speaks to the experiences of several Western nations, and the Alberta context, which is the focus of a more circumscribed research base. In my discussion, I draw on what the authors say about the effects

K.D. Gariepy, B.L. Spencer and J.-C. Couture (eds.), Educational Accountability:
Professional Voices From the Field, 35–48.

produced in other countries by school choice and accountability policies introduced in the 1980s and 90s. I then draw on what local scholars say about Alberta's unique school choice scene, especially in light of the advent of our own early-1990s reforms for both school choice and accountability. I provide a synthesis and discussion of the literature to highlight some of the key policy and practice effects of the reform programs. I conclude by offering considerations and possibilities for thinking about and avoiding some of the pitfalls of the school choice-accountability combination that have been particularly problematic in other countries. It is my hope that by offering the ideas herein, this chapter might initiate discussion among those in Alberta who are grappling with issues of school choice and accountability and their possible implications.

SCHOOL CHOICE AND ACCOUNTABILITY:
THE MAKINGS OF A QUASI-MARKET

Background and the Extra-local Context

The concepts of school choice and accountability are rooted in both liberal and conservative notions of public schooling and they are not new to the education systems of Western democracies. On one hand, choice policies are predicated on values of individual liberty and freedom (Ladd, 2003). Advocates of school choice uphold the autonomy of parents and contend that, as the primary educators of their children, they ought to have the right to choose from the widest possible range of educational options. On the other hand, accountability policies rest on the premise that the state should oversee all matters public, including education. In this sense, questions about the rights and responsibilities of individuals in the provision of schooling (i.e., accountable for what, to whom, and for what purpose?) are strongly linked to the larger aims and purposes of public education (Kogan, 1988; Stein, 2001). However, since the 1980s, a shift has occurred. According to Brown, Halsey, Lauder and Wells (1997), current accountability and school choice policies have emerged in New Right discourses that have prevailed in industrialized nations for the past quarter century: "New Right ... ideology couples a neo-liberal view of the virtues of individual freedom and the free market with a traditional conservative view that a strong state is necessary to keep moral and political order" (p. 19).

School choice and accountability policies are two key features of reforms that have been included in the broader public sector restructuring programs of the past two decades. First, neoliberal ideas about school choice theoretically construct parents and students as the market's consumers and position them as able to exercise individual freedom in selecting a school of their choice. Restricting access to education to the neighbourhood school alone is tantamount to the state usurping parents' natural rights. Second, while traditional views of accountability position schools as responsible for and answerable to the state's purposes of public education, the prevailing neoliberal infusion of private sector values into public sector operations has shifted the more conservative conceptions of accountability from "oversight" to "regulation" (Blackmore, 1988; Power, 1997). Neoliberal corporate dimensions "of consumer choice, of contract efficiency, quality, and capital ownership" (Ranson, 2003, p. 464) have introduced an altered and intensified form of accountability, which has been bolstered by the tenets of new public management (NPM). Adopted in much of the post-industrial world, NPM is characterized by a governance style that defines accountability through results, output targets, performance standards and the measurement of achievement (Gewirtz, 2002; Pal, 2006; Stitzlein, Feinberg, Greene & Miron, 2007).

Specific to education, public policies for choice and accountability are interconnected in the emergence of what has become referred to as the quasi-market. Le Grand and Bartlett (1993) define a quasi-market as a public sector system, intended to retain the aims of equity that have been characteristic of traditional public sector programs, while introducing free market mechanisms for the promotion of efficiency and effectiveness. There are differences between the free market and the quasi-market on both the supply and demand sides. West and Pennell (2002) explain these differences in their description of the UK public education reforms of the 1980s:

> In the case of schools there is therefore competition between the institutions for 'customers' (i.e. pupils or their proxies, their parents). However, in contrast to organisations in conventional markets, state schools are not profit-making. On the demand side, consumer purchasing power is not expressed in terms of money. Instead it takes the form of an earmarked budget restricted to the purchase of a specific service..... Reforms were designed to bring market forces into the school-based education system and to make it more consumer-oriented. The emphasis on consumer choice was anchored in an overarching belief in the superiority of market forces. (p. 207)

Together, quasi-market mechanisms, such as open attendance boundaries, per pupil funding arrangements and the public ranking of schools, construct a culture wherein schools compete for students (Leithwood, 2001). Leithwood (2001) identifies the market as a leading governmental approach to accountability.

Educational quasi-markets function according to some basic market assumptions. Parents and students, in the roles of "clients" or "consumers" and according to individual needs and desires, are able to make rational choices in the selection of a school. And, if they are not satisfied with the educational "product" with which they are provided, they can leave that school and choose another. It is further argued that this will inject a competitive vigour into a monopolistic public education system that has historically been characterized by schools with closed attendance boundaries. When no school is ensured a captive audience by a designated catchment area, the competition for enrolment will make schools more accountable to the customers they serve. Champions of choice contend that accountability is inscribed into the market system's very essence: schools that give parents and students what they want will make gains in enrolment, while those that do not will see their enrolments decline (McCluskey, 2005). Fear of losing students to competitors purportedly prompts schools to adjust and optimize the educational programs and "customer services" they provide (Gewirtz, 2002; Taylor, 2006; Waslander & Thrupp, 1995).

Understood this way, school choice in the quasi-market system is the accountability mechanism par excellence. However, as I stated in my introduction, in combination, accountability and school choice work in reciprocal ways, so the reverse is also true: accountability in the quasi-market system can also be understood as the school choice mechanism par excellence. This becomes the case in systems that have adopted NPM principles of accountability and thus employ mechanisms for output targets, quantifiable performance standards and measurements of achievement. Such results-oriented systems produce the "data" necessary for consumers to make informed and appropriate choices from among the various schools and programmes available.

Background and the Alberta Context

By the early 1990s, the neoliberal and NPM ideas that had found favour in other Western democracies had also taken root in Alberta (Kachur & Harrison, 1999). While in some jurisdictions in the province school choice policies had existed since the 1970s, they took on a new complexion as a result of the educational agenda introduced, beginning in 1993, by Premier Ralph Klein and the Progressive Conservative Party. In addition to massive budget cuts to public sector services and programs, included in the "Klein Revolution" were the following reforms:
- revenue collection from municipal school taxes was centralized at the provincial level and, subsequently, funds were redistributed to school boards based primarily on levels of enrolment
- schools received a "block" or lump sum for spending within provincial guidelines and provision for site-based management was made
- local school control and decision-making was to be achieved through the formation of school councils, consisting of students, parents, community representatives, teachers and principals
- provision for charter schools, an alternative to the public school system, was announced
- parental choice was promoted through a system where funding "followed" the student and schools were funded according to the number of students enrolled
- to enhance accountability, key performance indicators were established for administrative and instructional purposes and schools were required to report information regarding parent and student satisfaction and student results on standardized tests
- the Province's testing program was expanded to be more comprehensive, including Provincial Achievement Tests (PAT) in core subjects for grades 3, 6, and 9 and diploma exams in core areas for grade 12 (Bruce & Schwartz, 1997; Spencer, 1999).

Over the years, while contested to varying degrees, most of these reforms have taken hold such that neoliberal, NPM principles now permeate Alberta's school system and are, for the most part, accepted as the "new normal." In the current policy framework, funding and accountability are interconnected in the Renewed Framework for Funding School Jurisdictions (Alberta Education, n.d.), which has, as one of its three pillars, accountability. The accountability pillar (Alberta Education, 2009) is designed to give "school boards the flexibility and freedom to meet the unique needs of their students and communities." Specifically, as per the reformed funding scheme, a fixed amount of funding follows each child in the form of a basic instructional grant (or credit enrolment units in the case of high schools) that is allocated directly to the district and, in turn, to the school in which the student is enrolled. In short, the higher the enrolment, the more money a school gets. Accountability is to be ensured through the public reporting of academic achievement scores and satisfaction surveys.

Combined, the research on the Alberta scene (Bosetti, 2004; Maguire, 2006; Taylor 2006; Taylor & Mackay, 2008) provides a clear picture of how school choice policies interact with accountability policies in a way that generates an educational quasi-market. Since schools seek the coveted educational grants that follow students, they are compelled to appeal to potential consumers through marketing their "product," evidence of which is readily available in the form of the accountability pillar data. Under these conditions, competition among schools ensues, and innovation and diverse programming flourishes as individual schools attempt to carve out niche markets for themselves or appeal to the predilections of certain potential consumers. School administrators, supported by policies of decentralization and site-based decision-making, are regarded as having the tools necessary to make changes to boost the popularity of their schools and enhance the quality of education provided. Thus, they are also deemed responsible for the learning outcomes of students (Bruce & Schwartz, 1997) and, ultimately, schools are "to be more accountable to the public by demonstrating improvement in student achievement scores" (Bosetti, 2004, p. 400).

While Alberta's provincial legislation and regulations allow school districts to develop policies promoting school choice, these provisions have been taken up in jurisdiction-specific ways and to varying degrees. The city of Edmonton provides a powerful example of how school choice and accountability operate together to reinforce a quasi-market system. School choice in Edmonton is not a new phenomenon. Since the mid-1970s, Edmonton Public Schools has operated according to a "choice" model (Edmonton Public Schools [EPS], 2008). Since the reforms, however, the Edmonton Catholic School District has also opened its school boundaries, albeit with some restrictions (Edmonton Catholic School District [ECSD], 2008) and, as both the city's major school boards respond in significant ways to what the choice legislation allows, Edmonton has become a flagship for public school[i] choice. Indeed, the city is seen as a living laboratory for studying school choice policies (Maguire, 2006; Taylor, 2006; Taylor & Mackay, 2008). In recent years, this has become especially true because of the surge of newly created alternative focus programs. What school choice means in practice is that, if they wish and if space and programming allow, students and parents are encouraged to enrol in a school outside of their immediate catchment area. This also means that the school districts vie for students and that schools within each district compete to keep enrolments at optimal levels. Angus McBeath (2007), a former EPS Superintendent, explains school choice as follows:

When we started our effort to try to make the system more responsive to its customers, we opened up all the schools in the system to every kid. Today in 2006, 57 percent of students ... will go somewhere in the system, but they will not go to their home school. And we provide subsidized passes on the city's transportation system to make sure kids from ages 5 to 19 can access any school in the system. To make it even more attractive to attend our system, we have about 35 "programs of choice" dotted throughout the city in multiple locations. I would reckon about 40 percent of Edmonton students attend a "program of choice." A program of choice might be Chinese language and culture. It could be performing arts; it could be science and technology; it could be a form of methodology like project-based learning; it could be a military academy; it could be a hockey school; it could be a school of French immersion; it could be Christian education, Jewish education, Arabic education and culture; it could be whatever parents want. (p. 2)

According to McBeath (2007), the EPS choice system has intensified as a result of Alberta's school choice legislation:

If we didn't offer [programs of choice], the parents would collaborate and develop a charter school. Our goal in Edmonton Public Schools is to make sure there are no private or charter schools. It's the Legislature of Alberta that decided that they would fully fund charters and partially fund private education.... The rest of the school districts in the province said, "Let's kill the legislation," and we said, "Let's out-compete the private schools and charter schools, so that no one will want to go there." And not only that, there are now virtually no charter or private schools in metro Edmonton.... The three mother ships of the private school business in Edmonton all asked to join us. (p. 2)

What is especially interesting to me is the strengthened link between school choice and accountability that is evident in McBeath's (2007) explanation of "keeping schools 'on their toes'"

What do we do with the weak schools that parents don't want to send their kids to? Well, I say there are two things: You can make the school better, or you can shut it. We had a school in Edmonton that was designed for 1,300 kids; there were only 300 left. A thousand parents already closed this school by moving their children to other schools. That hadn't occurred to people.... in my view, what closed the school was the failure of the school to retain the children either through a lack of good programming or through a lack of good discipline or better teaching. It's not magic keeping a school open in our city: You just have to do a good job.... It's not an innovation in Edmonton in 2006 to have school choice. It's just the way we operate. We do not use the word "privatization"; we do not use the word "competition"; we just want to keep our schools on their toes. (p. 3)

Specific to accountability, McBeath (2007) talks about "providing information to parents:"

.... I can tell you that parents will send their kids to a bad school sometimes, even though they have a choice to go with another school. So we decided we would have to start a very rigorous system of measuring student achievement — and not just measuring it, but reporting it.... We also measure annually parent, staff and student satisfaction with the performance of the system as a whole and with each individual school. Every year our parents, staff and students participate in an anonymous survey by school on everything from their satisfaction and confidence in their principal to their satisfaction and confidence in the safety of their children to the quality of the teaching.... All of the results are published annually, and schools set targets to improve the levels of satisfaction in each of these areas every year, or at least key areas every year. (pp. 4–5)

Given the above explanation of Alberta's education quasi-market, it appears that, at least in the case of EPS, a school's primary chain of accountability is no longer upward to the district or ministry; rather, it is downward to the consumer. Those such as McBeath (2007), who advocate choice systems, applaud this development. However, this apparent inversion of accountability "direction" does not mean that the school district administration and the provincial ministry of education are no longer bodies to which the school is held accountable. The accountability pillar mechanisms, especially standardized test results and satisfaction surveys, as well as enrolment trend analyses, still provide "upward" information about the degree to which the school is not only accountable to ministry expectations, but also accountable and attractive to its customers. Thus, in Alberta, a certain conception of accountability can be seen to operate throughout the system; it is channelled through the labyrinth of the enrolment choices and expressions of satisfaction that are made by the quasi-market's chief agents: parents and students.

EFFECTS OF THE SCHOOL CHOICE-ACCOUNTABILITY COMBINATION

As was explained in the previous section, the quasi-market is intensified by the combination of provincially mandated school choice and accountability policies (Cookson, 1994; Gewirtz, 2002). While many argue in favour of such a combination (Chubb & Moe, 1990; McBeath, 2007), others contend that, when accountability systems are imposed alongside choice systems, the market culture that ensues can undermine the potential benefits that the choice programs have to offer. Thus, the limits of market forces in public spheres, such as education, are revealed (Stein, 2001). In the following, I draw on the research conducted both outside of and in Alberta to outline some of the effects of the school choice-accountability combination.

It has been observed that the education quasi-market introduces an entre-preneurial ethic and mindset into schools. As in private enterprise, concerns about survival, market share, outward appearance and image become paramount as schools are held accountable for the size of their student body, and they therefore must attract additional students and retain those already enrolled (Gerwitz, Ball, & Bowe, 1995; Robenstine, 2000). This can become a preoccupation, especially for administrators in undersubscribed schools (Gewirtz, et al., 1995; Gewirtz, 2002). As a result, school leaders may resort to visible promotional activities that highlight a school's satisfaction rates, academic achievement levels or a variety of other performance measures (Oplatka, 2002). Involvement in open houses, feeder school/daycare visits, the delivery of handbills, the posting of road signs and myriad other tactics become the stock components of a robust marketing strategy designed to bring students through the front doors. Lubienski (2005) argues that there is some evidence, however, to suggest that while many schools are responding to the pressures of both school choice and accountability policies by engaging in activities meant to enhance a school's competitive position, the various promotional strategies do not leverage substantive school improvement efforts. Thus, it is important to assess how schools are truly responding in the competitive milieu rather than uncritically accepting the logic of the market. As Gerwitz et al. (995) argue, it is clear that quasi-market forces do not, by definition, translate into the survival of pedagogically superior schools and the demise of inferior ones, as many school choice proponents suggest. Rather, concerns over accountability often spark the introduction of powerful and sophisticated school marketing schemes that can undermine any inherent benefit a choice program may have to affect school success on the basis of genuine merits, such as improved student achievement.

Albeit to different degrees and depending on the school jurisdiction, the effects outlined above are mirrored in Alberta. Here, the strategies employed appear to be in response to measures for which schools are held accountable, for example, increasing enrolment to generate additional funding, attracting a certain type of student to boost the school's test score averages, or enhancing the cumulative reputation of the school through highlighting client satisfaction. Through his study of Edmonton schools, Maguire (2006) gained some important insights into how school leaders respond under quasi-market circumstances. Public relations strategies included, among others, television and radio ads, large message boards on busy streets, feeder school visits, making daycare contacts, school newsletters (some of which were translated into the languages of diverse communities), door-to-door mail drops and even home visits. Some schools re-examined and diversified their programmes to include offerings such as full-day kindergarten and International Baccalaureate programs. Maguire suggests that, in Edmonton, "choice is less about driving unsuccessful schools out of business and more about adapting to meet the needs of students, parents and community" (p. 78).

However, Taylor & Mackay (2008) challenge claims that Edmonton's alternative programs have emerged in response to families' preferences and consumer demand. They argue that it is the school districts that have played the key role in constructing program ideas and creating demand for the alternatives they prefer to offer. The use of the sanctioned accountability discourse "of responding to diverse needs" merely lends "legitimacy to practices aimed at increasing the district's student population" (p. 558). That is, new alternative programs are offered in neighbourhoods where school enrolments are dropping due to shifting community demographics. This is more a result of government pressure on districts to increase their utilization rates than it is an attempt to meet the needs of students (Taylor,

2006). As Maguire (2006) notes, for example, "situated in a highly competitive environment, Edmonton is an ideal case study for understanding school choice through the lens of declining enrolment" (p. 51). Likewise, in her study of another large urban school district in Alberta, Bosetti (2004) found that alternative programs were actually engineered by the district, and were not created to meet any particular demand. What the research suggests is that the implementation of alternative programs in Alberta's choice system is more a reaction to policies that tie levels of funding to levels of enrolment than it is a response to the educational needs and desires and, therefore, demands of parents.

It must also be remembered that in the Alberta context, while curricular and programme diversification is promoted, students are still required to participate in a provincial standardized testing program. Given this key mechanism to which school leaders are held accountable, it is not surprising that they often focus on the provincial achievement test scores (Maguire, 2006). This external accountability pressure is compounded by the Fraser Institute policy think tank's regular publication of a ranked listing, according to PAT and diploma exam results, of all schools in Alberta. As Taylor (2006) argues, due to these pressures, school leaders not only want to reduce their numbers of low-achieving students, they also want to "attract and retain more academically focused students" (p. 43). By extension, the choices out-of-boundary students actually have may be diminished as some "students are regarded as more valuable than others" (p. 44). To attract the desirable clientele, schools will often reinvent themselves by adopting a new focus geared toward high achievers, hiring teachers with special expertise, developing partnerships with elite institutions such as universities and modernizing their facilities (Taylor, 2006). It is evident that the school choice-accountability combination inspires the development of a marketable product – an undertaking for which much administrative time and effort is typically devoted (Maguire, 2006).

DISCUSSION

Positioned on the balcony, trying to discern what is happening down on the dance floor (Heifetz & Linsky, 2002), I realize that school choice itself may not necessarily be problematic. Rather, the difficulty seems to be located in the context that emerges when a choice policy functions in concert with a high-stakes accountability framework. Specifically, accountability mechanisms related to standardized achievement test results and to attracting students and funding implicate school choice in a quasi-market. In Edmonton, choice was a feature of public education well before the reforms of the early 1990s. Since then, the introduction of legislation that officially codifies school choice, a new funding scheme and an accountability framework featuring achievement test and satisfaction survey results has intensified competition. As McBeath's (2007) account suggests, school leaders are now placed in a position where they feel compelled to market their schools within a competitive culture.

I believe that a society's education system holds a mirror to itself. If we, in Alberta, do not thoughtfully and critically engage in the quasi-market, I wonder whether we will like what we see staring back at us. Sahlberg's (2008) summation and caution are, I think, appropriate to the Alberta context:

> Pressure for competition, higher productivity, better efficiency and system-wide excellence are also having visible affects on schools and teachers. Schools that compete over students and related resources are shifting their modus operandi from moral purpose towards production and efficiency, i.e. measurable outcomes, higher test scores and better positions in school league tables. Increasing public sector productivity is changing small, personalized schools into larger institutions that are characterized by opportunity and choice but rarely by personal care and collective responsibility (p. 4).

As Gerwitz et al. (1995) explain, the very notion of school marketing gives rise to key concerns. First, elevating self-presentation and image to the forefront of school leaders' consciousness represents a significant cultural transformation in schooling. This has important implications for resource and energy allocation, the nature and integrity of relationships and the way schools are managed. Second, marketing changes what is valued in schools. Third, schools become beholden to new incentive structures that encroach upon their culture and shared meanings. It is clear to me why these concerns are important. Seemingly, quasi-markets challenge the spirit of community cohesion, solidity and harmoniousness that schools have traditionally aimed to foster. Further, when the culture, values and relationships of a school system are altered, the integrity of the "public" in public education is challenged. Unmistakably, there are tensions between the values underpinning market economics and public education (Davies & Quirke, 2005; Gewirtz, 2002) and we need to be mindful of the values on which we focus. Indeed, a discussion of school choice and accountability is not merely an academic exercise; it is inherently connected to broader questions about public education and the kind of society we hope to build.

Hess (2002) argues that the nature of schooling and the way it is provided makes it a poor fit for the market model. In a marketized environment, democratic imperatives can be displaced and eroded by capitalistic imperatives in, for example, arrangements where the student-school relationship is reconceptualized as a consumer-producer transaction (Ben Jaafar & Anderson, 2007). This trans-formation represents a triumph of neoliberal, competitive values and a displacement of education's moral purpose. As Cookson (1994) asserts, education is not a morally neutral, contracted commodity, and market rationalities, born of the choice and accountability combination, often come into conflict with the moral purposes of education. In this regard, Dempster, Freakley and Parry (2001) ask: Do the ideals of the marketplace furnish what can be deemed appropriate to satisfying collective values? The ideal that propels quasi-markets is competition, yet competition is incompatible with the values that reside at the heart of public education's moral purpose, which, in part, is to create a mutual and negotiated democratic society in which citizens regard each other as collaborators and cooperators, not competitors. The business ethos that the school choice-accountability combination draws education into corresponds to a marginalization of the moral, social and public foundations in which teaching and learning are rooted (Oplatka, 2002; Woods, Woods & Gunter, 2007; Sahlberg, 2008). It is an ethos within which inequality and social stratification are not only tolerated, but exacerbated (Ball, 1993; Waslander & Thrupp, 1995). This is especially disconcerting for those who work on the assumption that a more egalitarian society is a healthier society (Waite, Boone & McGhee, 2001).

Notwithstanding these observations, if one were to assume that school choice is in Alberta to stay, where might we look to find another model that is not driven by neoliberal notions of the market, wherein a regulatory kind of performance-based accountability plays such a key role? Cambridge Public Schools (CPS) in Massachusetts might provide an example. Though not perfect, in 1980 this school district implemented a controlled choice plan that skillfully integrates a genuine concern for the democratic values of fairness and accessibility. It makes conscious efforts to ensure that its education system does not simply reproduce and further entrench existing class stratification. Specifically, CPS has established a series of measures to help ensure equitable access. For example, a district-run Parent Information Centre oversees and centralizes registration, thus taking enrollment decisions out of the hands of site-based administrators who, the district worried, may have a vested interest in steering "undesirable" students to other sites because of accountability concerns. The decisions made by district-level personnel account for parents' desires but also seek to balance individual school populations along lines of race, gender, special needs and, most notably, socioeconomic status (Cambridge Public Schools, 2001).

While the CPS school choice model is premised on notions of democracy and equity, whether or not it would work in Alberta is questionable given our powerful accountability framework. It might offer a viable alternative, but in light of the effects I have outlined above, it is likely that some of the more laudable aspects of the CPS plan would be undermined. In short, school choice policies, when put into practice along with the current, state-imposed accountability framework, become highly influenced and affected by the quasi-market forces of competition that work against some key principles of equitable and democratic public education.

CONCLUSION

In the United States, the National Working Commission on Choice in K-12 Education (2003) commented that "there is nothing automatic about choice.... Choice's outcomes, for good or ill, depend heavily on how communities structure and implement [them]" (p. 4). While I agree with this conclusion, I would add that what school choice becomes also depends on the other policies with which it interacts. I have taken the opportunity to step back from my day-to-day work environment as an urban Alberta principal and ask the question, "What is really going on here?" (Heifetz & Linsky, 2002). In doing so, I have seen how accountability policy can change how school choice is operationalized.

The link between accountability and school choice finds its expression in an education quasi-market, which, the research suggests, rests on a set of assumptions that should not be ignored: that school personnel will react to market pressures by concentrating their efforts on genuine school improvement, that the needs and expectations of parents and students will dictate what choices are made available, and that all participants in the market have the same conditions under which to exercise choice. However, as is evident in the literature, educators' energies are frequently channelled into marketing and image management instead of into bona fide school improvement efforts; it is often a school district's desire to attract students to undersubscribed schools that results in new and varied programs of choice; and the pressures of increasing school achievement test results can effect decisions about the desirability of potential clients and, therefore, the degree of choice actually available to all students. All of these effects are related to the power of a state-imposed accountability framework that, in actuality, is only loosely connected to the day-to-day operation of schools and the work that is involved in providing the kind of teaching and learning that is necessary for the best possible education for Alberta's students.

Accountability is fundamental and important to our educational and governance systems. However, when accountability policies are rooted in neoliberal and NPM ideals they become problematic, particularly when such policies operate alongside and, inevitably, in reciprocal ways with school choice policies. As I have outlined in this chapter, the effects of the school choice-accountability combination in Alberta may be more broad and far-reaching than is immediately apparent. Consequences may include a subtle but significant reengineering of public education and a shift in the very purposes of schooling that we have come to count on in building an equitable and democratic society.

NOTES

[1] In Alberta, historically, Catholic and Protestant "separate" schools have been publically funded and are therefore considered to be public schools.

REFERENCES

Alberta Education. (n.d.). *The renewed funding framework: Education funding for Alberta school jurisdictions: 2008/09 school year*. Retrieved March 7, 2009, from http://www.assembly.ab.ca/lao/library/egovdocs/2008/aled/168709.pdf

Alberta Education. (2009). *About the accountability pillar*. Retrieved February 10, 2009, from http://education.alberta.ca/admin/funding/accountability/about.aspx

Ball, S. (1993). Education markets, choice and social class: The market as a class strategy in the UK and the USA. *British Journal of Sociology of Education, 14*(1), 3–19.

Bartlett, W., & Le Grand, J. (1993). *Quasi-markets and social policy*. London: Macmillan.

Ben Jaafar, S., & Anderson, S. (2007). Policy trends and tensions in accountability for educational management and services in Canada. *Alberta Journal of Educational Research, 53*(2), 207–227.

Blackmore, J. (1988). *Assessment and accountability*. Geelong, Australia: Deakin University Press.

Bosetti, L. (2004). Determinants of school choice: Understanding how parents choose elementary schools in Alberta. *Journal of Education Policy, 19*(4), 387–405.

Brown, P., Halsey, A. H., Lauder, H., & Wells, A. S. (1997). The transformation of education and society: An introduction. In A. H. Halsey, H. Lauder, P. Brown, & A. S. Wells (Eds.), *Education, culture, economy, and society* (pp. 1–44). Oxford: Oxford University Press.

Bruce, C. J., & Schwartz, A. M. (1997). Education: Meeting the challenge. In C. Bruce, R. Kneebone, & K. McKenzie (Eds.), *A government reinvented: A study of Alberta's deficit elimination program* (pp. 383–416). Toronto: Oxford University Press.

Cambridge Public Schools. (2001). *Controlled choice plan*. Retrieved February 12, 2009, from http://www.cpsd.us/Web/PubInfo/ControlledChoice.pdf

Chubb, J., & Moe, T. (1990). *Politics, markets, and America's schools*. Washington, DC: Brookings Institute.

Cookson, P. (1994). *School choice: The struggle for the soul of American education*. New Haven, CT: Yale University Press.

Davies, S., & Quirke, L. (2005). Providing for the priceless student: Ideologies of choice in an emerging educational market. *American Journal of Education, 111*(4), 523–547.

Dempster, N., Freakley, M., & Parry, L. (2001). The ethical climate of public schooling under new public management. *International Journal of Leadership in Education, 4*(1), 1–12.

Edmonton Catholic School District. (2008). *School boundaries or catchment areas*. Retrieved March 7, 2009, from http://www.ecsd.net/schools/boundaries.html

Edmonton Public Schools (2008). *Mission and philosophy*. Retrieved February 13, 2009, from http://www.epsb.ca/about/mission.shtml

Gewirtz, S. (2002). *The managerial school: Post-welfarism and social justice in education*. London: Routledge.

Gewirtz, S., Ball, S., & Bowe, R. (1995). *Markets, choice, and equity in education*. Buckingham, England: Open University Press.

Heifetz, R., & Linsky, M. (2002). *Leadership on the line: Staying alive through the dangers of leading*. Boston: Harvard Business School Press.

Hess, F. (2002). *Revolution at the margins: The impact of competition on urban school systems*. Washington, DC: Brookings Institution Press.

Kachur, J. L., Harrison, T. W. (1999). Education, globalization, and democracy: Whither Alberta? In T. W. Harrison & J. L. Kachur (Eds.), *Contested classrooms: Education, globalization, and democracy in Alberta* (pp. xiii–xxxv). Edmonton: University of Alberta Press.

Kogan, M. (1988). *Education accountability: An analytic overview* (2nd ed.). London: Hutchinson.

Ladd, H. (2003). Introduction. In D. Plank & G. Sykes (Eds.), *Choosing choice: School choice in international perspective* (pp. 1–22). New York: Teachers College Press.

Liethwood, K. (2001). School leadership in the context of accountability. *International Journal of Leadership in Education, 4*(3), 217–235.

Lubienski, C. (2005). Public schools in marketized environments: Shifting incentives and unintended consequences of competition-based educational reforms. *American Journal of Education, 111*(4), 464–486.

Maguire, P. (2006). *Choice in urban school systems: The Edmonton experience*. Kelowna, BC: Society for the Advancement of Excellence in Education.

McBeath, A. (2007, September 28). The Edmonton Public Schools story: Internationally renowned superintendent Angus McBeath chronicles his district's successes and failures. *Policy Brief*. Retrieved February 11, 2009, from http://www.mackinac.org/archives/2007/s2007-13.pdf

McCluskey, N. (2005, April 20). Corruption in the public schools: The market is the answer. *Policy Analysis, 542*. Retrieved February 11, 2009, from http://www.cato.org/pubs/pas/pa542.pdf

National Working Commission on Choice in K-12 Education. (2003). *School choice: Doing it right makes a difference*. Retrieved March 7, 2009, from http://www.brookings.edu/~/media/Files/rc/reports/2003/11education_fixauthorname/20031116schoolchoicereport.pdf

Oplatka, I. (2002). The emergence of educational marketing: Lessons from the experiences of Israeli principals. *Comparative Education Review, 46*(2), 211–224.

Pal, L. (2006). *Beyond policy analysis: Public issue management in turbulent times* (3rd ed.). Toronto: Thomson Nelson.

Ranson, S. (2003). Public accountability in the age of neo-liberal governance. *Journal of Education Policy, 18*(5), 459–480.

Robenstine, C. (2000). School choice and administrators: Will principals become marketers? *Clearing House, 74*(2), 95–99.

Sahlberg, P. (2008, April 18). *Real learning first: Accountability in a knowledge society*. Paper presented at the Symposium on Leadership in Educational Accountability: Sustaining Professional Learning and Innovation in Alberta Schools, Edmonton, AB.

Spencer, B. L. (1999). *An analysis of attitudes and beliefs about public education in Alberta*. Unpublished Master's Thesis, University of Calgary, Calgary, Alberta, Canada.

Stein, J. G. (2001). *The cult of efficiency*. Toronto: Anansi Press.

Stitzlein, S. M., Feinberg, W., Greene, J. & Miron, L. (2007). Illinois project for democratic accountability. *Educational Studies: Journal of the American Educational Studies Association, 42*(2), 139–155.

Taylor, A. (2006). 'Bright lights' and 'twinkies': career pathways in an education market. *Journal of Education Policy, 21*(1), 35–57.

Taylor, A., & Mackay, J. (2008). Three decades of choice in Edmonton schools. *Journal of Education Policy, 23*(5), 549–566. doi: 10.1080/02680930802192774.

Waite, D., Boone, M., & McGhee, M. (2001). A critical sociocultural view of accountability. *Journal of School Leadership, 11*(3), 182–203.

Waslander, S., & Thrupp, M. (1995). Choice, competition and segregation: An empirical analysis of a New Zealand secondary school market, 1990–93. *Journal of Education Policy, 10*(1), 1–26.

West, A., & Pennell, H. (2002). How new is New Labour? The quasi-market and English schools 1997 to 2001. *British Journal of Educational Studies, 50*(2), 206–224.

Woods, P., Woods, G., & Gunter, H. (2007). Academy schools and entrepreneurialism in education. *Journal of Education Policy, 22*(2), 237–259.

PATRICIA GERVAIS

4. ACCOUNTABILITY AND THE INDIVIDUAL PROGRAM PLAN

Accountability has become a major feature of special education systems in many Western industrialized nations. As Bottery (2000) argues, in a global community, "the social is subordinated to the economic. . .the state increases its control of policy steerage, . . .and [educators'] . . . fundamental role is as implementers of government policies" (p. 20). For educators faced with an array of accountability instruments, questions about *what* one is accountable *for* and to *whom* one is accountable reflect the observation by Ranson (2003) that "the complexity and multilateral nature of 'accountable' relationships. . .denies any simple linearity of answerability" (p. 461). In special education, the individual program plan (IPP) is a policy text that incorporates accountability on a variety of bureaucratic and interpersonal levels. In this chapter, I will show how two approaches to accountability are merged in special education and, in particular, how they are operationalized through the process of the IPP. First, I will provide two definitions of accountability discussed by Ben Jaafar and Anderson (2007) and show how they relate to my discussion of the IPP as an example of multi-dimensional accountability in special education. Next, I will review special education literature and documents that relate to the IPP and accountability in special education. Using data from focus group discussions conducted by the Alberta Teachers' Association (ATA), I will then provide a synthesis of how teachers in Alberta see and understand the IPP. Finally, I will conclude that, in Alberta, the IPP serves a dual purpose as both a learning document and a tool for accountability. The intent is to create the opportunity for reflection on the assumptions, guiding principles and realities that form the background of the IPP and to consider how these factors impact both the work of teachers and the provision of education programs for students with exceptional needs.

ECONOMIC-BUREAUCRATIC AND ETHICAL-PROFESSIONAL ACCOUNTABILITY

Ben Jaafar and Anderson (2007) provide two orientations that are particularly useful when looking at accountability in special education. The first, *Economic-Bureaucratic Accountability* (EBA) emphasizes *outcomes*. In this framework, teachers are individually accountable to an external audience (e.g., the public, the Ministry of Education) to provide results-based evidence of the efficient and effective use of public funds. What counts as evidence is that which can be both observed and measured, and this is reported in quantitative terms, whenever

K.D. Gariepy, B.L. Spencer and J.-C. Couture (eds.), Educational Accountability:
Professional Voices From the Field, 49–58.

possible. Relating this view to special education, teachers are responsible to the public and the Ministry to provide evidence of the achievement of students, including those with exceptional needs. Further, given the costs associated with the education of students with special needs, school and district administrators are accountable for how such dollars are spent. The second orientation, *Ethical-Professional Accountability* (EPA) emphasizes educational *processes* and the outcomes that are achieved as a result of these. In this arrangement, educational accountability is seen in terms of ethical and moral obligations. Teachers both accept and share collective responsibility with other stakeholders for the advancement of democratic principles. Such principles, based on values such as participation, trust, reciprocity, and self-actualization, are not easily reported using outcomes-based language. Pertaining to accountability in special education, EPA describes in part the standards that teachers hold for themselves as both individuals and a profession. These two multi-dimensional, simultaneously occurring and competing orientations create tensions for teachers because they respond to a variety of external and internal forces of accountability in their daily work.

THE INDIVIDUAL PROGRAM PLAN

The *Individual Program Plan* (IPP) outlines an education plan for a student with exceptional needs. It has the functions of managing the overall instructional goals of a student, communicating these goals in written form between all parties involved in the student's program and accounting for the student's progress towards identified goals (Mercer & Mercer, 2001). The components of the IPP include student demographics and the identification of members of the student's learning team; an overview of student strengths and needs; assessment data; general accommodations to the student's learning environment; specific goals and objectives to be addressed in the program; strategies towards the achievement of these goals and objectives; regular review of progress towards stated goals and objectives; and a transition plan. The IPP is not meant to be a detailed, individual curriculum but addresses key areas of development for an individual student during a school term.

The IPP is an example of a document that satisfies both EBA and EPA. First, it is a bureaucratic document responsive to legislation and held up as evidence of an effective education for the student with special needs. Second, it is a professional document that involves ethical and instructional concerns for meeting the learning needs of the student. To the latter end, it defines an education plan and communicates this plan among members of a student's learning team. As Krumins (2009) asserts,

it is true that by simply completing the document, having parents sign it and reviewing it at the end of reporting periods, we educators have complied with our legal responsibility. But the individual education plan is an ethical responsibility as well. It is a tool that is intended to benefit the student. (p. 12)

The IPP emerged over a period of time that saw changes in the delivery of educational services to students with special needs across North America – a move from institutionalized placements into mainstreamed settings and finally inclusive environments. The impetus for these changes may be traced to the Education for All Handicapped Children Act (1975). This American law established the right of access for students with special needs to a free and appropriate public education that would be regulated by an individualized education plan. Access to a free and appropriate public education was further defined with reference to the *least restrictive environment,* which meant that, as much as possible, students with mild special education needs should be served in settings with typically developing peers. As a result of this legislation, mainstreaming emerged as a system including both regular education and a range of part- and full-time special education placements. Although Canadian education is a matter of provincial jurisdiction, a similar trend developed across Canada.

It would be difficult to discuss issues relating to the IPP without reference to inclusive education. Calling for students with severe disabilities to be included in regular classrooms whenever possible, inclusion evolved from the mainstreaming movement of the 1980s and early 1990s. Inclusive education was also influenced by a movement in the United States known as the Regular Education Initiative, which argued that a dual education system was unnecessary and that most students with special needs could be served in the regular classroom. Timmons and Wagner (2008) point out that inclusion has also become a priority in Canadian society, as demonstrated by the Speech from the Throne of February 2nd, 2004: "We want a Canada in which citizens with disabilities have the opportunity to contribute to and benefit from Canada's prosperity – as learners, workers, volunteers and family members" (p. 3). Inclusive education supports the premise that both students with disabilities and their typically developing peers benefit socially when they are educated in inclusive environments that reflect the richness and diversity of society.

A number of legislative and other related documents currently provide guidelines for the provision of special education in Alberta. Section 47(10) of the School Act (2000) states that "a board may determine that a student is, by virtue of the student's behavioural, communicational, intellectual, learning, or physical characteristics, or a combination of those characteristics, a student in need of a special education program." The *Standards for Special Education* (Alberta Education[AE], 2004) and the *Information Bulletin on Standards for Special Education, Amended June 2004* (AE, 2007) outline further regulations with respect to access, appropriateness, accountability and appeals for students with mild, moderate, or severe disabilities or for those who are gifted and talented. The *Handbook for the Identification and Review of Students with Severe Disabilities 2008/2009* (AE, 2008) specifies the documentation required and thus qualifies and standardizes those students who will receive funding for special education programming. An IPP is required for each student identified with an exceptional need. Guidelines and strategies for individualized program planning as well as a number of examples are found in *Individualized Program Planning* (AE, 2006).

Collectively, these documents provide a set of bureaucratic standards and expectations for special education practice and the IPP.

HOW EDUCATORS IN ALBERTA UNDERSTAND THE IPP

As front line creators and implementers of the IPP and those who interact most frequently with special needs students, teachers present a strong professional voice regarding both the intended and the actual functions of the IPP. With concerns about these functions, in 2007, the Alberta Teachers' Association (ATA) decided to investigate the IPP in relation to teacher workload. Two actions taken as a result were a survey on the teaching and learning conditions of students with special needs and a series of focus group discussions conducted around the Province. The survey was distributed to members of the ATA's Special Education and Gifted and Talented Specialist Councils who attended Council conferences in their respective areas. The 263 respondents were not randomly selected and do not accurately portray a representative sample of special educators; however, as a group, they may be representative of a range of teaching professionals involved in special education. The results of the survey were compiled and used for discussion in the focus groups. Approximately 135 rural and urban educators voluntarily participated in these discussions, which lasted for two to three hours. Approximately 58% reported that they were classroom teachers, but the groups also included teachers with classroom and administrative duties, administrators at the school or central office level, substitute teachers and others. Each group was provided with a brief background of the project and the ARA resolution before they reviewed survey results by focusing on three goals: (a) identifying the things that help or hinder the development and implementation of IPPs, (b) identifying things that schools, jurisdictions, the ATA, Alberta Education and universities can implement to assist with the development and implementation of IPPs and, (c) making recommendations to the larger group of participants. Working with the raw data from these discussions, I identified seven broad themes that will be discussed in the next section. These themes offer a contextualized perspective on the realities of writing and implementing the IPP in Alberta.

Theme 1: Professionalism and Trust

Based on the data from the focus groups, it appears that educators perceive the IPP as a formal document that both accompanies and articulates a professional process. Administrative support, at both the school and district levels, was seen as a particularly important factor in the successful writing and implementation of IPPs. Collaboration with other teachers, through activities such as learning team conferences and professional learning communities, was also seen as a key source of support for the IPP. Trust was a significant sub-theme of this category, as suggested by many teachers' expressed desires to have their professional competence in successfully completing and implementing the IPP more highly valued by others involved in the education of students with special needs (e.g., school and district administrators, Ministry officials and parents). The importance of trust was also articulated in the need for better communication about provincial and district policies concerning the IPP and the transfer of student information through cumulative files, as well as better communication with parents.

Parental involvement in the IPP process was seen as both a positive factor and a challenge. For example, parental support in writing and implementing the IPP was viewed by many participants as being constructive; on the other hand, some concerns were also expressed that parents' expectations of the IPP are sometimes too high and/or unrealistic and that some parents have difficulty supporting or following through on goals set out in the IPP. Some participants also noted that the format of the IPP document itself is perceived by some parents as unfamiliar and not user-friendly.

Theme 2: Students

Data from the focus groups also suggests that educators believe the IPP should be primarily focused on the student. Comments related to the IPP such as, "it professionalizes what teachers are doing to help students," it "provides insight [in]to [the] behaviour needs of students," it "communicates student strengths" and "it helps to set goals with students" all point to the importance of this theme. At the same time, however, many areas of concern were also raised:
- Some participants felt that the voice of the student is under-represented in the IPP process, as suggested by the comment: "How does the student feel about how the IPP support helped him or her?"
- Some participants expressed dissatisfaction with the current system's emphasis on areas of deficit and its lack of attention to the educational needs of a range of diverse learners.
- Some participants identified that the size and composition of classes can create unbalanced learning opportunities for students. Some noted that the quality of educational programming is compromised, particularly when there is inadequate teacher support, in large classes that include a high proportion of special needs or high behavioural needs students. As a result, participants urged administrators and policy makers at all levels to give additional consideration to the implications of class size and composition when placing students with special needs.
- Some participants voiced broad educational and life goals for students with special needs and suggested that the IPP should "focus on transitions and future goals from the onset of a student's education."
- Some participants implied that there is a disconnect between special education and mainstream education, particularly with respect to curriculum and assessment. Several teachers noted that the focus on content and timelines introduced by Provincial Achievement Tests (PATs) is not inclusive of students with special needs. Suggestions for improvement included more focus on process and performance-based assessments and better opportunities for students to work and demonstrate their learning at their own paces. Regarding the PATs, suggestions included that less emphasis be placed on these tests; that more

opportunities for success be provided for students experiencing difficulty succeeding on these tests; that schools should not be penalized for students who do not write the tests; and that consideration be given to reviewing or possibly discontinuing these tests.

- Some participants suggested that there is a lack of consistency around the concept of inclusion. For example, some indicated that there should be more placement and program options for students with special needs. This concern was primarily expressed by participants from rural settings but was also shared by some participants from urban settings.

Theme 3: Training

Many participants in the focus group discussions indicated a need for more training in writing and implementing the IPP. With respect to writing, they stated their need for more guidance in areas such as coding, wording, formatting, writing measurable goals and objectives (i.e., SMART goals) and using information from other specialists and resources effectively. Some participants suggested that a large portion of the necessary training could occur through school-based professional development activities such as inservices, workshops, mentorship programs and professional learning communities. Many teachers suggested that new teachers in particular require support when faced with programming for students with special needs. Teachers also identified a need for knowledgeable special education personnel at all levels, but particularly in the schools. Universities were seen as an important contributor for improving the level of special education knowledge in schools. Participants made a number of suggestions pertaining to teacher education programs, including: mandatory special education courses; specific courses on topics such as writing the IPP, differentiated instruction and provincial special education policy; incentives to increase enrollment in special education programs; and further educational opportunities for practicing teachers.

Theme 4: Time

Lack of sufficient time was seen as the greatest inhibitor to effectively writing and implementing the IPP. Sufficient time is not only needed to write an IPP for each student with exceptional needs, but to collaborate with other teachers and parents, to involve students (where appropriate), to satisfy standards for writing the IPP, to meet with specialists (e.g., speech-language pathologists, occupational therapists, psychologists) and paraprofessionals, and to track student progress towards identified learning goals. Many teachers also noted that even in schools where there is personnel assigned to oversee special education, these individuals often lack sufficient time to carry out their duties and to work closely with classroom teachers. In addition to providing more time overall for writing and implementing the IPP and meeting with others, participants suggested that more training, a streamlined and improved IPP format and additional clerical support would be helpful.

Theme 5: Specialized Supports

The importance of specialized supports to facilitate the effective formulation and implementation of the IPP also emerged as a key theme in focus group discussions. These supports included: inter-agency collaboration; access to, timely and meaningful feedback from specialists; time to meet with specialists; access to relevant print and electronic resources; and processes to coordinate information from various sources. Teachers also identified a number of existing, helpful support personnel at the jurisdiction and school levels who already contribute to successful IPPs, including special education coordinators, support teachers, resource teachers, counsellors, classroom support teachers and instructional assistants. Where these individuals were perceived as having adequate training and time to carry out their supporting roles, they were deemed helpful to classroom teachers.

Theme 6: Funding

Many participants expressed concerns with current levels of special education funding and related this concern to other areas that support effective programming, such as time, class size and composition and staffing. The cost of assessments and consultations, inadequate professional time for writing the IPP and collaborating with others, insufficient opportunities for professional development, inadequate resources and supports for students with mild or moderate needs, and the challenges associated with students with behavioral needs or complex issues were all listed as areas that might be improved if more funding for special education was available.

Theme 7: Accountability

The final theme emerging from my analysis of the focus group data relates to accountability. While it is clear that participants recognized the potential of the IPP to operate as an instrument of accountability in many levels of the education system (e.g., school, district and Ministry), it is also apparent that, based on statements made in the focus groups, participants are also concerned that the IPP sometimes functions as an end in itself, rather than as a means to an end. In other words, as a result of various and competing accountability-related expectations, the IPP, as a working document, can constitute a distraction from the special education programming it was designed to guide and support. For example, a significant number of comments suggest that participants believe the IPP process lacks consistency and clarity; that IPP-related goals become too numerous and/or too lengthy; that the IPP duplicates parts of the report card; and that IPP completion is a generally onerous task. To address these concerns, several participants suggested that the Ministry, school districts and the ATA collaborate to design and implement a simplified, standardized, Web-based IPP document template. This suggestion may have been related to a desire to expedite the completion and updating of the IPP; allow teachers to complete it with more confidence; integrate a variety of already Web-based special education resources, such as goals, objectives, and strategies; and facilitate consultation, collaboration and communication among members of the student's learning team. As Mercer and Mercer (2001) point out, it might also help teachers and other members of the learning team to manage and monitor records and academic progress in real-time.

Given the simultaneous expression of a desire for greater trust and professional empowerment regarding the completion and implementation of the IPP, it is surprising that some participants were also interested in further standardization. On one hand, they suggested that the IPP, as an already highly standardized account. ability instrument, has resulted in more work and stress for classroom teachers; on the other hand, they also called for its increased standardization and computerization. The potential danger is that increased standardization can contribute to the EBA structures and practices that interfere with the pedagogical and ethical purposes of the IPP.

THE IPP AS A TOOL FOR ACCOUNTABILITY AND A LEARNING DOCUMENT

In an effort to provide effective policies that ensure high quality opportunities for exceptional students, the IPP has become a highly standardized document. Meyen and Skrtic (1995) argue that standardization is an organizing principle of education wherein schools are operated and managed as though they were machine bureaucracies, which assign specific standardized tasks to workers for the efficient and effective creation of a final product. Meyen and Skrtic's view reflects the notions of economic-bureaucratic accountability (EBA) that I have drawn upon in this chapter. However, as I have also argued, the IPP reflects the notions of ethical-professional accountability (EPA) as well; it depends on professional competence and commitment to the welfare and education of students. Specifically, the IPP serves as both an EPA blueprint for an individual education program and EBA evidence of the effective use of resources to support such programming. Because the IPP is a function of how EBA and EPA approaches exist in Alberta's public school system, this document and the standards and practices it operationalizes must be recognized as reflecting the multi-dimensional nature of educational accountability.

Indeed, the research findings I have presented in this chapter point to the importance of seeing the IPP as a tool that is responsive to both EBA and EPA demands. The key question, however, is: If we accept that this multi-dimensional concept of accountability is appropriate for understanding the realities of special education, to what degree do some dimensions of accountability become highlighted while others are minimized and, as a result of this tension, in practice, does the IPP enhance the quality of educational programming for students with special needs?

A review of the themes I used to organize the research data reveals the significant degree to which participants talked about the work of special education and the role of the IPP as tied to the ethical-professional dimensions of accountability. Here, noteworthy are six out of seven of the themes: professionalism and trust, students, training, time, specialized supports and funding. With the exception of one remark related to the need for more technical training for completing the IPP, all comments for all themes focus on ethical-professional dimensions of the educator's role in meeting the needs of exceptional students. The comments emphasize the importance of instructional processes, the need for sufficient and appropriate time and resources, the key role of professional expertise along with

the value of teamwork for the shared and collective responsibility for educating students. All themes can be understood to reflect the democratic principles of inclusive education, especially student participation and self-actualization. It is clear that participants would interpret educational accountability in terms of the ethical and moral obligations and responsibilities of educators. In this sense, the EPA function of the IPP is to provide instructional guidance; it can be understood as a learning document.

The sixth theme, accountability, reflects participant concerns about the bureaucratic function of the IPP and the degree to which it was considered to be problematic. It reveals the difficulties inherent in reporting progress and outcomes in standardized terms and in providing sufficient evidence of the efficient and effective use of funds. It also reflects how the individualized, tedious and time-consuming work of the IPP is seen as a distraction from what is most important – meeting the educational needs of children. Even the suggestion for a Web-based IPP interface that is more streamlined and standardized was a response to a desire to complete the documentation as expediently and thoroughly as possible in order to focus on more important educational matters. In this sense, the IPP meets EBA demands; it is acknowledged as a tool for accountability.

The research suggests that, when factors such as adequate resources and support from other professionals, administrative and parental support, class size and composition, training, professional development, and professional empowerment are not addressed, the economic-bureaucratic function of the IPP becomes onerous, and the quality and effectiveness of individual programming for students may be adversely impacted. However, a well-designed, succinct and user-friendly IPP could provide clarity and purpose to a student's education, and can be helpful in organizing instructional activities and reporting on student progress. Thus, while serving the demands of economic-bureaucratic accountability, the IPP can maintain its focus on the ethical-professional dimensions of accountability that address the needs of the exceptional student.

The issues identified by the participants in the focus group discussions are not new in the area of special education. They underscore the notion that forces of economic-bureaucratic and ethical-professional accountability continue to affect special education practice. Speaking at a recent special education symposium, MacKay suggested that what is needed in special education is a "lighthouse of equality" as a guide for educators (personal communication, May 8 & 9, 2008). By offering different ways to think about accountability and presenting research findings about the effects of the introduction of state-mandated special education policy into an already complex and challenging educational environment, this chapter offers new ways to think about a public education system that recognizes the dimensions of accountability that are most appropriate and relevant to maintaining a lighthouse notion of special education which is reflective of a just and equitable society.

REFERENCES

Alberta Education. (2004). *Standards for special education.* Retrieved February 16, 2009, from http://education.alberta.ca/media/511387/specialed_stds2004.pdf

Alberta Education. (2006). *Individualized program planning.* Retrieved February 16, 2009, from http://education.alberta.ca/media/525567/ipptitle.pdf

Alberta Education. (2007). *Information bulletin on standards for special education, amended June 2004.* Retrieved February 16, 2009, from http://education.alberta.ca/media/309101/3.2.8.pdf

Alberta Education. (2008). *Handbook for the identification and review of students with severe disabilities 2008/2009.* Retrieved February 16, 2009, from http://education.alberta.ca/media/841679/hdbk_severedisabilities_2008–2009.pdf

Ben Jaafar, S., & Anderson, S. (2007). Policy trends and tensions in accountability for educational management and services in Canada. *Alberta Journal of Educational Research, 53*(2), 207–227.

Bottery, M. (2000). Educational policies: The global context. In M. Bottery (Ed.), *Education, policy, and ethics* (pp. 1–26). London: Continuum.

Education for All Handicapped Children Act of 1975, Pub. L. No. 94-142. Retrieved February 17, 2009, from http://thomas.loc.gov/cgibin/bdquery/z?d094:SN00006:@@@D&summ2=m&|TOM:/bss/d094query.html

Krumins, J. (2009). *12 ways to make individual education plans useful and meaningful.* Retrieved March 26, 2009, from https://www.autismaspirations.com/index.php?option=com_content&view=article&id=5:12-ways-to-make-individual-education-plans-useful-and-meaningful&catid=2:articles&Itemid=6

Mercer C. D., & Mercer, A. R. (2001). *Teaching students with learning problems.* Upper Saddle River, NJ: Merrill Prentice Hall.

Meyen, E. L. & Skrtic, T. M. (Eds.). *Special education & student disability: An introduction, traditional, emerging, and alternative perspectives.* Denver, CO: Love Publishing.

Meyen, E. L., & Skrtic, T. M. (Eds.). (2001). *Special education & student disability: An introduction, traditional, emerging, and alternative perspectives.* Denver, CO: Love Publishing.

Ranson, S. (2003). Public accountability in the age of neo-liberal governance. *Journal of Education Policy, 18*(5), 459–480.

School Act, R.S.A. c. S-3 (2000). Retrieved February 17, 2009, from http://www.qp.gov.ab.ca/documents/Acts/s03.cfm?frm_isbn=9780779733941

Timmons, V., & Wagner, M. (2008, June). Connection between inclusion and health. *Health & Learning Magazine.* Retrieved March 26, 2009, from http://www.ctf-fce.ca/e/publications/health_learning/default.asp?doc=Issue6&noid=13

5. ALLEVIATING TEACHER ALIENATION

Sustainable, Distributed Leadership and
Capacity for Putting Accountability into Perspective

Alberta Education's accountability framework emphasizes large-scale, standardized testing and satisfaction surveys and is criticized for being an imposed, top-down mechanism that diminishes the role of the professional teacher in making appropriate decisions about student learning and assessment (Alberta Teachers' Association [ATA], 2006). In this chapter, I discuss alienation as a negative consequence of the pressures teachers experience while working within government-mandated accountability regimes (Couture & Liying, 2000; Runte, 1998; Taylor, Shultz, & Wishart Leard, 2005). I suggest that sustainable, distributed leadership may alleviate teacher alienation by developing school capacity at both the organizational and individual levels. This, in turn, can result in positive outcomes for student learning and success.

CONTEXT

In the early to mid-1990s, as part of a larger programme of educational reforms, Alberta adopted new funding and accountability systems. With regard to teachers' work and professionalism, there are two effects of these reforms that are important to note. First, to a great extend, funding for programs and services to support classroom teachers and their professional development was cut. Second, centralized control, in the form of outcomes-based curriculum and standardized provincial achievement tests and diploma exams, was strengthened. Accountability measures, in particular, have attributed to the intensification of teachers' work (Taylor, et al., 2005). Couture and Liying (2000) argue that, as a result, a growing sense of dislocation, remoteness and alienation is having an impact on the sense of efficacy teachers feel in their role in Alberta schools.

TEACHER ALIENATION

Kesson (2003) discusses alienation in terms of the negative impact that the market economies of Western capitalism have had on the way individuals understand themselves in relation to their work. She argues that this kind of alienation is being experienced by teachers as a result of workplace conditions wherein actions and the ability to use discretionary judgement are limited and constrained as a result of the strong influence of high-stakes testing programs and outcomes-based

K.D. Gariepy, B.L. Spencer and J.-C. Couture (eds.), Educational Accountability:
Professional Voices From the Field, 59–65.
© *2009 Sense Publishers. All rights reserved.*

accountability systems. Tye and O'Brien (2002) define teacher alienation as a combination of feelings of isolation, powerlessness and meaninglessness. While they define alienation somewhat differently, they agree with Kesson's findings that teacher alienation is widespread and, in many cases, is cited by teachers as a sufficient cause for leaving the profession. Indeed, their study revealed that participants who had already left the profession ranked accountability mechanisms (i.e., curriculum standards, high-stakes testing and test preparation) as the number one reason for leaving.

Speaking of the externally imposed educational reform program of the early 1990s in the UK, Ball (1994) offers the following account of teacher alienation:

> Separately and together these changes are bringing about profound shifts in the nature of teaching and the teachers' role ... and profound shifts in the nature of schools as work organizations; not surprisingly, many teachers appear weary and wary, stressed and depressed, alienated and bitter. They are faced with threats to their autonomy and status.... And in a sense the more successful they are at coping, the more of themselves as professionals and their experience they must forgo.... Together these changes assert a massive and complex technology of control over teachers' work in all its aspects. (pp. 11–12)

King (2007) and Stitzlein et al. (2007) also argue that a misplaced confidence in the power of accountability mechanisms to produce accountable schools and teachers fails to give sufficient weight to the importance of teachers' expertise and their ability to make the necessary judgments that are required in the classroom and for recognizing the individual needs of students. Hargreaves (1994) agrees, suggesting that large-scale reforms and accountability systems have undermined professional autonomy and have resulted in teachers' feelings of alienation.

In his later work, Ball (2001) writes about teacher alienation in relation to what he refers to as "performativity." He comments on the extent to which those in educational institutions are required to perform and to produce and respond to the performative information that is central to organizations regulated by new accountability and audit policies. He cites two aspects of performativity that contribute to teacher alienation. First, he refers to inauthenticity: "the alienation of self is linked to the incipient 'madness' of the requirements of performativity: the result, inauthentic practice and relationships" (p. 215). Second, he refers to the "splitting" that can happen when teacher "commitment, judgement and authenticity within practice are sacrificed for impression and performance. There is a potential *splitting* between the teacher's own judgements about 'good practice' and students' 'needs' on the one hand and the rigours of performance on the other" (pp. 214–215).

Similarly, in Alberta, Couture and Liying (2000) and Runte (1998) describe the culture of performance that has been produced by the province's large-scale standardized testing programs. According to Couture and Liying (2000), "the examinations have served to place teachers under continued monitoring and surveillance by administrators, superintendents, and parents who equate 'public accountability' of what teachers do with performance on the provincial examinations" (p. 65). As teachers' sense of professional autonomy is eroded and as their work becomes intensified and divorced from what they understand to be purposive and meaningful, stress and alienation occur. As the research shows, alienation is one of the consequences of the implementation of top-down, imposed accountability policies.

The ATA (2006) argues that the substantial resources necessary to support current accountability policies would better serve students if allocated to developing school-level capacity through teacher support that, in turn, would support more meaningful and constructive local strategies for assessing student learning and the effectiveness of curriculum and teaching. Thus, instead of external accountability, internal accountability is necessary. This, I argue, is achievable through sustainable, distributed leadership practices which are fostered in professional communities through strong personal and organizational capacity. Further, distributed leadership arrangements and vital school-level capacity have the potential to alleviate teacher alienation.

SUSTAINABLE, DISTRIBUTED LEADERSHIP

Hargreaves (2009) points to the need for sustainable leadership and suggests that the government reform programs for which current accountability systems have been developed "bypass leadership altogether and go straight to the classroom through teacher-proof and leader-proof programs of prescribed delivery" (p. 33). In this sense, "leadership is the afterthought of educational change" (p. 33). Sustainable change, Hargreaves (as cited in ATA, 2008) argues, requires sustainable leadership:

> A commitment to sustainable leadership must move us beyond the micro-management of standardization, the crisis management of repetitive change syndrome and the all-consuming obsession with higher performance standards at any cost into a world where we can bring about authentic improvement and achievement for all children that matters, spreads and lasts.

Hargreaves also calls for distributed leadership, which "draws change out of staff, rather than driving reforms through them. It is integral to curriculum and pedagogical development more than reform implementation and incompatible with meeting imposed targets related to external initiatives" (p. 35).

Harris and Spillane (2008) offer a definition of distributed leadership perspective that incorporates the following points:
– recognises that there are multiple leaders and that leadership activities are widely shared within and between organisations....
– focuses upon the interactions, rather than the actions, of those in formal and informal leadership roles....
– is primarily concerned with leadership practice and how leadership influences organisational and instructional improvement....
– acknowledges the work of all individuals who contribute to leadership practice, whether or not they are formally designated or defined as leaders....

– central to system reconfiguration and organisational redesign which necessitates lateral, flatter decision-making processes. (p. 31)

Harris and Spillane draw on the work of other scholars in the development if this definition to also acknowledge that there is significant overlap between the concepts of distributed leadership, collaborative and participative and teacher leadership:

> A distributed view of leadership 'incorporates the activities of multiple groups of individuals in a school who work at guiding and mobilizing staff in the instructional change process'. It implies a social distribution of leadership where the leadership function is stretched over the work of a number of individuals where the leadership task is accomplished through the interaction of multiple leaders. (p. 32)

I argue that sustainable, distributed leadership is a viable solution to teacher alienation because it offers possibilities for change to the ways that individuals participate in discussions and decisions about teaching and learning and about accountability. When principals and teachers can effectively balance the demands for school improvement through distributed and sustainable leadership, quality instruction and professional development can become a focus and teachers can improve their practice. Thus, with increased expertise they are able to make unique leadership contributions (Printy & Marks, 2006). In this way, professional autonomy can be reinforced and teacher alienation can be addressed.

As I have argued above, sustainable, distributed leadership offers one approach to alleviating teacher alienation. It can also contribute to strong local-level school capacity (Harris, 2001; Stitzlein et al., 2007). Here, I use "capacity" in two ways: individual capacity and organizational capacity (Spencer & Freeman, 2005). Individual capacity relates to person's knowledge, skills, and dispositions (Newmann, King, & Youngs, 2001). It also involves self-efficacy, a person's perception of their own capacity to accomplish goals (Leithwood et al., 2001). It is developed by utilizing the knowledge, skills and dispositions of the collective and it depends on organizational arrangements that create flexible and sustainable processes for learning and relationship building (Mitchell & Sackney, 2000; Newmann et al., 2001).

Both individual and organizational capacity building depend on collaborative efforts and shared responsibility for outcomes (Lambert, 2006). These are the premises of distributed leadership. Specifically, through distributed leadership, organizational capacity is built through a focus on action, not on roles, and through the interactive work of many leaders, both formally and informally designated. It is developed through practices that support organizational and instructional improvement and through sharing the responsibility for decision making and for the outcomes and consequences of the decisions.

Distributed leadership also promotes organizational capacity because of its emphasis is on local, school-level practices that will result in increased student achievement and school improvement. This, along with all other features outlined above, is also important to developing individual capacity. Specifically, in distributed leadership models, teachers are key actors in collaborative processes. They are recognized as having professional expertise and as being capable of sharing leadership responsibilities and practices. They are considered to be capable of making suitable choices for their own professional development. They are key to the creation of appropriate curriculum and instruction and, because they are the ones closest to a school's students, they are given authority and are trusted to develop improvement plans and programs that will best meet the specific needs of the children in their classrooms and the wider school community (Leithwood & Earl, 2000). In this way, teachers are able and, indeed, expected to exercise autonomy. In turn, their personal capacity is built through the knowledge, skills, and dispositions they develop through distributed leadership and, as a result, confidence is increased and self-efficacy becomes strong.

DISCUSSION

Sustainable, distributed leadership and organizational and individual capacity work together at the school level to empower teaching professionals by bringing them back into the conversations and decisions about what affects them as professionals and about what affects and promotes successful instruction for student growth and positive educational experiences for all children (Hargreaves, 1997). In this regard, conversations about accountability and the work towards the development and practice of internally focused assessments, curriculum standards, and appropriate related professional development become the shared work of all leaders of the school, especially teachers.

In this vein, the ATA (2006) also offers leadership recommendations for a more effective accountability model that acknowledges the goals of distributed leadership and capacity. It focuses on the idea that "each education partner is accountable for those areas of the system within its authority and expertise" (p. 88). To address the top-down accountability model in use, Stitzlein et al. (2007) recommend that the teaching profession put school achievement test results into perspective by considering them against insights gained through professional training and expertise and by concentrating on "local knowledge" (p. 143) – the practical wisdom teachers gain in context. In this way, as Leithwood and Earl (2000) suggest, the goals of accountability can be achieved authentically through "increas[ing] the power of teachers in school decision making while holding teachers more directly accountable for the school's effects on students" (p. 13). By appropriately placing power and responsibility in the hands of teachers in schools, the alienating effects of accountability mechanisms, such as standardized curricula and large-scale testing, can be decreased and prevented.

CONCLUSION

By drawing together the scholarship on the alienating effects of externally-driven accountability policies and practices and the literature on sustainable, distributed leadership and its connection to organizational on individual capacity in schools, I argue that teacher alienation can be lessened and curtailed. The effects of working in a highly stressful and regulated performance culture and of having little autonomy, especially as regards accountability, will be less prevalent in contexts where sustainable, distributed leadership is valued and practiced for both organizational and individual capacity. Furthermore, through models for strong distributed leadership and heightened capacity, teachers, with confidence and professional autonomy, take a proactive leadership role in the provision of quality education. As Harris (2006) argues, school achievement can be positively correlated to the degree of distribution of leadership and, as Printy and Marks (2006) suggest, "when instructional quality moves steadily in an upward direction, student learning is likely to follow a parallel path" (p.131).

REFERENCES

Alberta Teachers' Association. (2006). *Accountability in education*. Edmonton, AB: Author.

Alberta Teachers' Association. (2008). *Leadership in educational accountability: Sustaining professional learning and innovation in Alberta schools* [Brochure]. Retrieved February 16, 2009, from http://www.teachers.ab.ca/SiteCollectionDocuments/ATA/Features/2007-08/Sustaining%20Professional%20Learning%20and%20Innovation%20in%20Alberta%20Schools.pdf

Ball, S. J. (1994). *Education reform: A critical post-structural approach*. Buckingham, England: Open University Press.

Ball, S. J. (2001). Performativities and fabrication in the education economy: Towards the performative society. In D. Gleeson & C. Husbands (Eds.), *The performing school: Managing teaching and learning in a performance culture* (pp. 210–226). London: RoutledgeFalmer.

Couture, J. C., & Liying, C. (2000). Teachers' work in the global culture of performance. *Alberta Journal of Educational Research, 46*(1), 65. Retrieved from the CBCA database.

Earl, L., Levin, B., Leithwood, K., Fullan, M., Watson, N., Torrance, N., et al. (2001). *Watching and learning: OISE/UT evaluation of the National Literacy and Numeracy Strategies: Second annual report*. Toronto: Ontario Institute for Studies in Education, University of Toronto.

Hargreaves, A. (1994). *Changing teachers, changing times: Teachers' work and culture in the postmodern age*. New York: Teachers College Press.

Hargreaves, A. (1997). *Beyond educational reform: Bringing teachers back in*. Buckingham, England: Open University Press.

Hargreaves, A. (2009). The fourth way of change: Towards an age of inspiration and sustainablity. In A. Hargreaves & M. Fullan (Eds.), *Change wars*. Bloomington, IN: Solution Tree.

Harris, A. (2001). Building the capacity for school improvement. *School Leadership and Management, 21*(8), 261–270.

Harris, A., & Spillane, J. (2008). Distributed leadership through the looking glass. *Management in Education, 22*(1), 31–34.

Kesson, K. (2003). *Alienated labor and the quality of teachers' lives: How teachers in low-performing schools experience their work*. Retrieved from the ERIC database.

King, D. (2007). School principles: How should we shape our education system? A former Minister weighs in. *Alberta Views, 10*(7), 32–35.

Lambert, L. (2006). Lasting leadership: A study of high capacity schools. *Educational Forum, 70*(3), 238–254.

Leithwood, K., & Earl, L. (2000). Educational accountability effects: An international perspective. *Peabody Journal of Education, 75*(4), 1–18.

Leithwood, K., Jantzi, D., & Steinbach, R. (1999). *Changing leadership for changing times*. Buckingham, England: Open University Press.

Mitchell, C., & Sackney, L. (2000). *Profound improvement: Building capacity for a learning community*. Lissa, Netherlands: Swets & Zeitlinger.

Newmann, F. M., King, M. B., & Youngs, P. (2001). Professional development that addresses school capacity: Lessons from urban elementary schools. *American Journal of Education, 108*(4), 259–299.

Printy, S. M., & Marks, H. M. (2006). Shared leadership for teacher and student learning. *Theory into Practice, 45*(2), 125.

Runte, R. (1998). The impact of centralized examinations on teacher professionalism. *Canadian Journal of Education, 23*, 166–181.

Spencer, B. L., & Freeman, S. (2005, July 2). *Examining the situation and capacity effects of the changing role of Ontario administrators and of their removal from the Ontario Secondary School Teachers' Federation.* Paper presented at the Linking Research to Professional Practice Institute, Calgary, AB.

Stitzlein, S. M., Feinberg, W., Greene, J., & Miron, L. (2007). Illinois project for democratic accountability. *Educational Studies: Journal of the American Educational Studies Association, 42*(2), 139–155.

Taylor, A., Shultz, L., & Wishart Leard, D. (2005). A new regime of accountability for Alberta's public schools. In T. W. Harrison (Ed.), *The return of the Trojan horse: Alberta and the new world (dis)order* (pp. 236–253). Montreal: Black Rose Books.

Tye, B., & O'Brien, L. (2002). Why are experienced teachers leaving the profession? *Phi Delta Kappan, 84*(1), 24–32. Retrieved from the Academic Search Complete database.

ALANNA CRAWFORD

6. ALBERTA'S *DISTRIBUTED LEARNING STRATEGY AND IMPLEMENTATION PLAN* AND CONCEPTIONS OF LEARNING AND EDUCATION DELIVERY

Alberta Education's (2008b) *Ministry Business Plan* states that its mission is to "inspire, motivate and provide the necessary tools and opportunities for every child to attain the knowledge, skills and attributes required for lifelong learning, self-sufficiency, work and citizenship" (p. 2). The Ministry recognizes that recent changes in society, such as student population diversity, family structure, knowledge about how students learn and increased use of technology have impacted teaching and learning in the early 21st century. It calls for change that will ensure that Alberta will "remain a leader in education, nationally and internationally" (p. 3). This is reflected in *Alberta's Distributed Learning Strategy and Implementation Plan: Draft 10* (Alberta Education, 2008c), which seeks to address these changes through a series of "priority actions" consisting of "measurement frameworks" and "outcomes" to be implemented by 2013. This document demonstrates a movement toward increased ministerial control and an emphasis on a skills-based education through computer-mediated distance learning delivery.

The focus of the work of the Distributed Learning Project Sponsor, Project Director, Advisory and Steering Committees, Project Team and Expert Working Groups is to implement the Ministry's mission for distributed learning:

> Alberta is committed to learner success through the development of collaborative and sustainable relationships that allow choice, flexibility, and authentic learning experiences. This includes a variety of resource formats, delivery mediums and strong teacher influence that allow learning and teaching to be individualized and independent of time and place. (Alberta Education, 2008c, p. 5)

When implemented, the Ministry's mission, enacted through *Alberta's Distributed Learning Strategy and Implementation Plan: Draft 10* (hereafter referred to as the *Strategy and Plan*), will significantly impact expectations of teachers, students and learning. However, despite what is articulated in the above quotation, in this chapter, I argue that the conceptualizations of learning and education delivery that underpin the *Strategy and Plan* do not acknowledge notions of broad and deep learning and the educational approaches necessary to help ensure that various delivery media and appropriate supports for student learning are practiced in K-12 distance learning in Alberta.

K.D. Gariepy, B.L. Spencer and J.-C. Couture (eds.), Educational Accountability:
Professional Voices From the Field, 67–77.

I contend that student learning is at the core of distributed learning and that its complexities and nuances must be recognized. With this focus, I draw on Delors et al.'s (1993) explication of the *four pillars of education* to define learning. These pillars provide a framework for my analysis and critique of the text of the *Strategy and Plan*. Specifically, I examine the text of this document in terms of conceptualizations of learning and of educational delivery.

COMPETING CONCEPTIONS OF LEARNING

Hargreaves and Fink (2006) argue that "learning is a preparation for life" (p. 32) and they refer to an understanding of the purpose of life as "our greater hunger" (p. 33). Through their elaboration of Delors et al.'s (1993) *four pillars of education*, they suggest that this hunger may be satiated:
- "Learning to know" involves the acquisition of knowledge and development of intellectual curiosity, which enables individuals to be life-long learners.
- "Learning to do" includes the acquisition of applied skills, the competence to put the skills into practice, the ability to collaborate effectively with others and being adaptive and creative when problem solving.
- "Learning to be" involves development and knowledge of the whole self (emotional, spiritual, moral, ethical, aesthetic, intellectual and physical) to achieve a healthy balance in life.
- "Learning to live together" requires developing an understanding, respect, empathy and concern for others by interacting and engaging in dialogue with those from diverse and similar frames of reference.

Before moving to the *Strategy and Plan*, I examine the Ministry's (Alberta Education, 2008a) broad definition of student learning:

> Students will be able to meet the provincial graduation requirements and be prepared for entry into the workplace or post-secondary studies. Students will understand personal and community values and the rights and responsibilities of citizenship. Students will develop the capacity to pursue learning throughout their lives. Students also should have opportunities to learn languages other than English and to attain levels of proficiency and cultural awareness that will help to prepare them for participation in the global economy. (p. 1)

The goals for a basic K-12 education are similar to the values of learning presented by Delors et al.'s (1993) *pillars*. To elaborate, Alberta's *Guide to Education* (Alberta Education 2008a) presents twenty *student learning outcomes* of a basic education, which offer guidance to educational stakeholders. Each of these outcomes may be authentically categorized within the *pillars*. For example, outcome (j) states that students will "recognize the importance of personal well-being and appreciate how family and others contribute to that well-being" (p. 1). This exemplifies the *learning to be pillar*. Outcome (r) states that students will "demonstrate initiative, leadership, flexibility and persistence" (p. 2). This reflects the *learning to do pillar*. Both examples illustrate that the deep, broad learning suggested by Hargreaves and Fink (2006) is also valued by the Ministry for K-12 education in Alberta.

The Ministry's *Guide* (Alberta Education, 2008a) also states that "to maximize student learning, programming needs to be flexible and responsive to the learning progress of students ... and students' learning needs" (p. 4). As Hargreaves and Fink (2006) contend, learning must be personalized to the "meanings, prior knowledge, and life circumstances of each student experiencing it" (p. 39). Furthermore, when learning is personalized, students respond to the authentic care and concern demonstrated by engaging enthusiastically in the learning process. The *Guide* offers direction in this matter: "Flexible programming involves using a broad range of instructional strategies to provide a variety of ways for viewing subject matter as well as an opportunity for individual students to learn in their preferred modes" (p. 4). It appears to indicate an understanding of authentic applications of the learning suggested by Delors et al. (1993). In the next section, I will analyse the policies outlined in the text of the *Strategy and Plan* (Alberta Education, 2008c) for further indications of authentic applications of the deep, broad learning outlined in the four pillars.

It is important to note that I generally support the *Guide's* definition for student learning because the broad vision for a basic education it presents corresponds to the deep, broad learning described in the *four pillars*. However, despite apparent congruencies between the *pillars* and the *Guide*, an analysis of the *Strategy and Plan* reveals that the congruencies are limited. On the surface, the *Strategy and Plan* seems to acknowledge the complexity and nuances of learning, but because learning has not been defined sufficiently, the statement has little substance. Its definition of distributed learning does not offer details about which personal understandings, knowledge, skills, abilities, or competencies students might gain while participating in distributed learning. It merely states that "distributed learning is a model which offers multiple channels of learning and teaching through a variety of delivery formats and mediums" and that "distributed learning includes all forms of learning" (Alberta Education, 2008c, p. 4). Specifically, the word "model" has various implications and connotations; it does little to clarify the meaning of "learning" in distributed learning. In addition, the broad statement, "distributed learning includes all forms of learning" does little to indicate authentic applications of the *four pillars*.

The rationale for the development of the *Strategy and Plan* states that "student-centred distributed learning is essential to fostering 21st century skills as it supports inquiry-based learning in and between classrooms, homes, communities and beyond" (Alberta Education, 2008c, p. 3). Underpinning such a statement is a particular conception of what learning *is* and what it is *for*. Because this framework is not transparent to all educational stakeholders, it is unclear what, in fact, "student-centred distributed learning" is. We are told that distributed learning is "essential to fostering 21st century skills," providing a clear indication of what distributed learning is *for* – the acquisition of marketable skills. This connection between the marketplace and the purposes of K-12 public education is evident in the neoliberal conception of education (Apple, 1998; Ball, 1994; Ranson, 2003, & Whitty, Power, & Halpin, 1998). Apple's description of current connections between the neoliberal marketplace and the purposes of public education is noteworthy:

> While a relatively close connection has always existed between the two, an even closer relationship now exists between the curriculum in our schools and corporate needs. In a number of countries, educational officials and policy makers, legislators, curriculum workers, and others have been subject to immense pressure to make the "needs" of business and industry the primary goals of the school system. The language of efficiency, production, standards, cost effectiveness, job skills, work discipline, and so on – all defined by powerful groups and always threatening to become the dominant way we think about schooling – has begun to push aside concerns for a democratic curriculum, teacher autonomy, and class, gender, and race equality. (p. 317)

Emphasizing the fostering of 21st century skills, the *Strategy and Plan* disregards the authentic applications of Delors et al.'s (1993) *learning to do pillar*, where effective, knowledgeable, creative, adaptive and collaborative application of skills are crucial. Therefore, when examining the *Strategy and Plan's* rationale in relation to this *pillar*, it seems somewhat simplistic in its suggestion that 21st century skills in general, rather than deep, broad learning are sufficient distributed learnings.

Additional marketable, 21st century skills that are emphasized in the *Strategy and Plan* are the acquisition and use of information and knowledge. In this case, the document reveals more about what learning *is* and *for*: "Our students' worlds are increasingly being shaped by their abilities to acquire, communicate, access and manipulate information while responding creatively to the demands of today's workplace" (Alberta Education, 2008c, p. 3). This statement suggests that information is a commodity to be acquired, but it does not acknowledge, as the *pillars* do, the importance of intellectual curiosity and the development of evaluative, analytical and critical thinking skills for gaining an independent point of view. For example, the abilities to retrieve, evaluate, critique and filter electronic information resources are essential for today's workplace, but these are not emphasized in this statement. When examined against the *learning to know* and *learning to do pillars*, the learning described in the *Strategy and Plan* seems narrow. The ability to acquire and manage information is emphasized as adequate preparation for participation in today's workplace.

In addition, the Ministry identifies its educational challenge for the future as follows: "to prepare students to participate as global citizens and be productive and innovative in the workplace of the future" (Alberta Education, 2008c, p. 3). This is a necessary goal, but it does not address the complexities involved in educating a global citizenry. Here again, Delors et al.'s (1993) *learning to live together pillar* provides a richer sense of global citizenship that entails "understanding of diversity and similarities among people, appreciation of interdependence, and the ability to engage in dialogue and debate to improve relationships, cooperate with others, and reduce violence and conflict" (p. 38). Moreover, although productivity and innovation are essential qualities for participation in the workplaces of today and the future, Delors et al. suggest that personal competence and interpersonal and social skills are also essential for success in the workplace. Specifically, their *learning to do pillar* emphasizes necessary "teamwork, initiative, readiness to take risks ... the ability to process information ... communicate with others and ... to manage and resolve conflicts" (Hargreaves & Fink, 2006, p. 37).

These examples demonstrate that, when compared to Delors et al.'s (1993) *pillars*, the learning described in the *Strategy and Plan* falls short in some important ways. In addition, as discussed earlier, although the *Guide to Education* echoes the learning to be pillar in several of its student learning outcomes (Alberta Education, 2008a), the *Strategy and Plan's* vision, mission, priority actions and outcomes do not reflect this *pillar*. The omission of outcomes that authentically address the kind of learning as described by Delors et al. (1993) points to the Ministry's reliance on conceptions of learning that emphasize skills for workplace preparation. These instrumentalist conceptions of learning are also more likely to rely on standardized practices for curriculum and assessment. As Hargreaves and Fink (2006) argue, these narrowing practices "may produce outcomes that have little enduring quality" (p. 40) and that do not acknowledge the deep, broad learning that they suggest will satiate our greatest hunger for an understanding of the purpose of life. With this limited and limiting focus, it is questionable whether the *Strategy and Plan* can offer the kind of learning support necessary as students endeavour to learn "in a deeper and broader sense that has lasting relevance for their present and future lives" (p. 40).

COMPETING CONCEPTIONS OF EDUCATION DELIVERY

Now that I have discussed competing conceptions of learning and the importance of deep and broad learning, I turn to a discussion of competing conceptions of education delivery to make explicit the ways in which the *Strategy and Plan* potentially asserts a centralized model of control over distance learning delivery that is based on notions of efficiency, standardization and accountability.

The *Strategy and Plan* (Alberta Education, 2008c) suggests that by acting individually and in isolation, Alberta school authorities have duplicated efforts in resource development and have not experienced success in collaborative professional development for distributed learning teachers or in offering students distributed learning options. While the *Strategy and Plan* indicates some interest in collaboration and shared control with various educational partners, the solution to the above problem is increased centralized control. That is, Alberta Education is to play a leading role in "optimizing existing distance learning and distributed learning services and in the setting of standards for distributed learning that better aligns the collaborative efforts of Alberta Education and those of School Authorities" (p. 18).

Through centralization, the neoliberal principles of efficiency, standardization and accountability are to be operationalized. For example, the discovery and definition phases of the *Strategy and Plan* include needs, risk and gap assessments; analyses of costs, risks, benefits and governance models; and an evaluation of the technical architecture necessary to deliver distance learning, all of which are to be implemented to help ensure the efficient use of resources. Further, with this emphasis on centralization and efficiency, the priorities of the *Strategy and Plan* are to systematically identify, define, communicate, approve, document and publish information reporting requirements and accountability measures for use by distributed learning schools. This focus on standardization for accountability and performance is exemplified in the curricula, wherein marketable, 21st century skills are stressed. Such an education, dominated by an instrumentalist commitment to preparing students for the workplaces of the global economy, may produce outcomes that are divorced from wider educational purposes (Hargreaves & Fink, 2006).

Although Alberta Education assumes the ultimate decision-making role and has power of approval over all projects, the *Strategy and Plan* appears to reveal a willingness to work "with school authorities and other stakeholders in the provision and development of resources, as well as in centralizing and expanding existing Alberta resource repositories" (Alberta Education, 2008c, p. 17). However, although the draft of the *Strategy and Plan* is a result of discussions and focus groups, it appears that schools offering print-based distributed learning courses were not adequately represented; therefore, valuable and constructive insights into the provision and development of print-based resources may have been overlooked.

The *Strategy and Plan's* focus on technology and digital delivery of distributed learning reflects the neoliberal influences on the Ministry's conceptions of the purposes of learning. That is, computers and technology are seen as appropriate to teaching and learning because, ostensibly, they provide students with the "skills that are necessary in the international competition for markets" (Apple, 1998, p. 315). As Apple points out, "educational officials and policy makers, legislators, curriculum workers, and others have been subject to immense pressure to make the 'needs' of business and industry the primary goals of the school system" (p. 317). The *Strategy and Plan's* emphasis on the technological delivery of distributed learning reinforces the idea that the primary purpose of learning is the acquisition of marketable skills. This does not reflect Delors et al.'s (1993) *learning to know* and *learning to do pillars*.

Furthermore, because more students take traditional, print-based distributed learning courses than online or digital-based courses (Alberta Distance Learning Centre, 2008), the omission of an important distributed learning delivery method that is often employed by students is noteworthy. It implies a lack of support for traditional distance education by correspondence. This is evidenced by the fact that future distributed learning resource development plans for grades 1 to 12 do not include print-only resources; all courses will incorporate an online and/or CD/ROM instructional component (J. Wiks, personal communication, May 14, 2008). This approach does not take into consideration the digital divide that exists between those who have readily available computer and Internet access and those who do not (Looker & Thiessen, 2003). Furthermore, there also exists a continuum of skills and preferences among students. For example, although many have grown up with digital technology and may be comfortable using computers and software for recreational purposes, they may not be comfortable with or wish to use computers as learning tools. In its failure to acknowledge the day-to-day realities of students who rely solely on print-based resources, the *Strategy and Plan* provides a further indication of how distributed learning is understood and of what the Ministry is willing to support.

Research suggests that ideally, only students who are autonomous, motivated learners should participate in distributed learning (Blaylock & Newman, 2005; Mupinga, 2005; O'Dwyer, Carey, & Kleiman, 2007). However, students of today may face various educational and demographic challenges, including remote and rural locations, small schools, large classes, budget constraints, bullying and threat of violence in schools, and teachers who lack adequate subject content knowledge. Blaylock and Newman (2005) suggest that these educational and demographic challenges may necessitate the enrolment of a range of learner types in distributed learning courses. It is also the case that students who do not meet "normal" academic requirements or who are required to repeat a course might be registered in distributed learning courses. These students, who are often considered to be "at risk," have already demonstrated learning difficulties and may require additional support to attain success. The *Strategy and Plan* suggests that it will increase "high school completion rates by providing students at risk of not completing school with additional opportunities to access basic education programs" (Alberta Education, 2008c, p. 6), but merely providing "basic education programs" will not effectively address the unique learning needs of all students. Neither will they effectively address the learning described by Delors et al.'s (1993) *four pillars*. Individualized student support structures are essential in the development of the whole self and in providing the interaction and dialogue often necessary for overcoming learning difficulties. Specifically, effective distributed learning support practices, such as reciprocal, deliberate student-teacher contact and effective school facilitation procedures, are not addressed. Although the document is intended to provide direction for implementation of distributed learning throughout the Province, the focus on what seems to be a narrow, standardized understanding of education delivery and the absence of specific discussions concerning student learning needs and student support practices raises questions about where students and student learning fit in the *Strategy and Plan*.

It is important to describe current assessment and accountability practices in Alberta before attending to a discussion of the *Strategy and Plan* in relation to innovative assessment practices. For the most part, Canada's current educational systems focus on structures of standardization, performance and accountability (Ben Jaafar & Anderson, 2007; McEwan, 2006). This is the case in Alberta, where a large-scale, standardized testing program dominates the province's educational accountability framework (Alberta Education, 2009). As the Alberta Teachers' Association (2006) points out, this is problematic because

> the tested parts of the core courses of mathematics, science, social studies and language arts are a fraction of the skills and knowledge students need to learn and of the values and predispositions they need to develop to be happy and productive members of society. (p. 75)

Although Alberta Education (2008c) officially states that its mission is to "inspire, motivate and provide the necessary tools and opportunities for every child to attain the knowledge, skills and attributes required for lifelong learning, self-sufficiency, work and citizenship" (p. 2), I argue that the emphasis on high-stakes testing suggests otherwise.

The effects of this emphasis have been well documented. For example, although standardized testing is often held up to be a fair method of evaluating student performance, results are often used to evaluate school and teacher effectiveness (Ben Jaafar & Anderson, 2007) and, as a result, instruction may focus on test-taking skills and aspects of curricula that might be tested on high-stakes exams. Furthermore, narrow, standardized curriculum assessments prohibit broad analyses of student learning that include performance on the basis of process, procedures and gaining understanding of essential concepts and critical thinking skills (Couture & Liying, 2000; Leithwood, 2001; Linn, 2003; Stitzlein, Feinberg, Greene, & Miron, 2007). Outcomes such as "good citizenship, social skills, technological competence, and preparation for employment" (Ben Jaafar & Anderson, 2007, p. 219) are not easily measured in current accountability systems. Stitzlein et al. (2007) concur, suggesting that "many of these socially and academically valuable traits are not currently measured by standardized tests, but rather require personal and ongoing interaction between student and evaluator" (p. 148). As a result, current accountability and high-stakes assessment practices do not allow application of professional or practical knowledge of individual student learning and personal needs (Stitzlein et al., 2007). For example, many students find high-stakes tests stressful and do not respond well when placed in these situations (Sahlberg, 2007; Stitzlein et al., 2007). Although students have opportunities to retake provincial exams, they are still held accountable for their own learning, even if they experience difficulty (Ben Jaafar & Anderson, 2007). High dropout rates and low participation in postsecondary schooling in Alberta might be results of these accountability policies, along with an associated lack of meaningful attention to and care for individual student's educational experiences (McEwan, 2006; Sahlberg, 2007).

The above effects of standardization and accountability are noteworthy. As Eisner (as cited in Hargreaves & Fink, 2006) warns, school systems "designed with an overriding commitment to efficiency may produce outcomes that have little enduring quality" (p. 40). This raises concerns in light of the fact that the *Strategy and Plan* is virtually silent on the subject of assessment and evaluation. Only one outcome of the *Strategy and Plan* mentions assessment, relating distributed learning standards to equity and consistency in meeting the learning needs of students (Alberta Education, 2008c). Given the importance that Alberta Education places on standardized testing and that the purpose of the *Strategy and Plan* is to align all distributed learning courses with the Alberta programs of study, it is possible that the Ministry sees no need to acknowledge practices that are alternatives or, at the least, complementary to standardized approaches. I argue that Delors et al.'s (1993) *four pillars* provide a more sophisticated description of education and educational success than is evident in current accountability and testing policies. For example, the tenets of the *pillars* are reflected in current, innovative assessment practices that offer a variety of promising approaches for distributed learning in K-12 settings. *Learner-centred assessment*, for instance,

> acknowledges that an important function of assessment is to facilitate and promote learning. It emphasizes the importance of assessing process (formative) as well as product (summative). Huba and Freed (2000) describe assessment as a process of "gathering information from multiple and diverse sources in order to develop a deep understanding of what students know, understand, and can do with their knowledge as a result of their educational experiences" (p. 8). This kind of assessment encourages purposeful dialogue, multiple discourses, collaboration, peer and self-evaluation, and contributes to a sense of community and shared purpose among a community of learners. (Comeaux, 2007, p. 1)

The *e-portfolio* also offers an alternative to current standardized assessment practices. The e-portfolio is a "digitized collection of artifacts, including demonstrations, resources, and accomplishments" made available via technologies such as Web sites, CD/ROMs and DVDs (Lorenzo & Ittelson, 2005, p. 2). E-portfolios are described by Lorenzo and Ittelson (2005) as "valuable learning and assessment tools" (Abstract) that are "helping students become critical thinkers and aiding in the development of their writing and multimedia communication skills" (p. 3) by providing opportunities for reflection, exchange of ideas and feedback.

Perhaps even more significant is the Ministry's choice not to demonstrate leadership in the implementation of such innovative assessment practices. Perhaps this indicates the insignificant value ascribed to the various formative assessments that distributed learning teachers make use of throughout the year. It might also indicate that innovative assessment practices are too complex to consider as a viable alternative to standardization. I argue that the *Strategy and Plan* offers the opportunity to include innovative assessment practices for distributed learning programs that support the deep, broad learning suggested in Delors et al.'s (1993) four pillars. Furthermore, the *Strategy and Plan* could include the framework and necessary technological infrastructure to support the establishment and storage of e-portfolios for all students. This would allow students to collaborate with peers in distributed and group settings. It would also provide increasingly mobile students with access to their portfolios anytime and anywhere and allow teachers of new students to assess current work based on past performance. Teachers might then assess student progress using self- and criterion-referenced evaluations, rather than by using the standardized testing procedures currently in place.

CONCLUSION

By examining *Alberta's Distributed Learning Strategy and Implementation Plan* in relation to Delors et al.'s (1993) *four pillars of education*, I have demonstrated that the *Strategy and Plan* addresses broad and deep student learning only superficially, and that it does not offer leadership in student support initiatives or innovative assessment practices. When one compares the Ministry's (Alberta Education,

2008b) stated mission for distributed learning with the language it uses to refer to its three-year plan, *Education Ministry Business Plan 2008-11*, the contradiction is clear. Teaching and learning have become a series of "priority actions, protocols, and outcomes" of a strategic business plan. Students seem to have become clients or customers to be served and evaluated in order to determine "evidence of success" (Alberta Education, 2008c, p. 8). I argue that the purposes of and the approach to education reflected in the *Strategy and Plan* are significantly different from those elaborated in Delors et al.'s (1993) *four pillars*. The broader goals and purposes of public education seem to be narrowed to economic, competitive and efficient objectives and simplistic, standardized, easily measured outputs (Sahlberg, 2008). The students graduating from this system may have the marketable skills necessary to perform efficiently in the workplace, such as "decision-making under uncertainty, just-in-time learning, information management, systems thinking, creativity and collaboration" (Alberta Education, 2008c, p. 3); however, as writers such as Sahlberg point out, although school jurisdictions around the world embrace market ideologies, broader, more sustainable goals of education, such as democracy and citizenship, are essential. While economic globalization and its consequent education reforms have roots in the neoliberal trends of the past century, this legacy continues in the narrow visions of the Ministry's *Strategy and Plan*: "Our challenge is to prepare students to participate as global citizens and be productive … in the workplace of the future" (Alberta Education, 2008c, p. 3). Similar to Sahlberg, Hargreaves (2009) also challenges this narrow focus of education, suggesting that "if schools and school systems sustain a broader vision, and express it in their teaching and curriculum, their students will become more interested in and committed to changing the world" (p. 18). Hak (2008) concurs, emphasizing that through deep and broad learning, this change can occur.

Finally, addressing, assessing, and evaluating student learning, as it is described by Delors et al.'s (1993) *four pillars of education*, presents both opportunities and challenges for distributed learning in Alberta. *The Strategy and Plan* affords the Ministry of Education the opportunity to offer students "deep and broad learning … that engages [them] in every sense – intellectually, socially, emotionally, and spiritually" (Hargreaves & Fink, 2006, p. 33). With innovative assessment practices becoming increasingly popular in schools and jurisdictions in Alberta, the *Strategy and Plan* further offers the Ministry the opportunity to lead the meaningful transformation of assessment and evaluation practices. Although Alberta Education's stated mission for distributed learning addresses these opportunities, the challenge lies in their application.

REFERENCES

Alberta Distance Learning Centre. (2008). *Percentage of coursework done by course, department, and delivery type.* Barrhead, AB: Author.

Alberta Education. (2008a). *Guide to education: ECS to grade 12.* Retrieved December 7, 2008, from http://education.alberta.ca/media/832568/guidetoed.pdf

Alberta Education. (2008b). *Education Ministry business plan 2008–11.* Retrieved May 8, 2008, from http://education.alberta.ca/media/779918/bp2008-11.pdf

Alberta Education. (2008c). *Alberta's distributed learning strategy and implementation plan: Draft 10.* Edmonton, AB: Author.

Alberta Education. (2009). *How the accountability pillar works.* Retrieved March 7, 2009, from http://education.alberta.ca/admin/funding/accountability/works.aspx

Alberta Teachers' Association. (2006). *Accountability in education.* Edmonton, AB: Author.

Apple, M. (1998). Teaching and technology: The hidden effects of computers on teachers and students. In L. Beyer & M. Apple (Eds.), *The curriculum: Problems, politics, and possibilities* (pp. 314–338). New York: SUNY Press.

Ball, S. J. (1994). *Education reform: A critical post-structural approach.* Buckingham, England: Open University Press.

Ben Jaafar, S., & Anderson, S. (2007). Policy trends and tensions in accountability for educational management and services in Canada. *Alberta Journal of Educational Research, 53*(2), 207–227.

Blaylock, T., & Newman, J. (2005). The impact of computer-based secondary education. *Education, 125*(3), 373–383. Retrieved from the Academic Search Complete database.

Comeaux, P. (2007). Assessment and learning: Applications in the online classroom. In G. Richards (Ed.), *Proceedings of World Conference on E-Learning in Corporate, Government, Healthcare, and Higher Education 2007* (pp. 238–240). Retrieved from the Education & Information Technology Library database.

Couture, J. C., & Liying, C. (2000). Teachers' work in the global culture of performance. *Alberta Journal of Educational Research, 46*(1), 65.

Delors, J., Al Mufti, I., Amagi, I., Carneiro, R., Chung, F., Geremek, B., et al. (1993). Learning: The treasure within: Report to UNESCO for the International Commission on Education for the Twenty-first Century: Highlights. Retrieved on May 10, 2008, from http://www.unesco.org/delors/delors_e.pdf

Hak, J. (2008, April, 14). Citizenship education must be part of every child's curriculum: Improving participation in democratic process calls for early start. *Edmonton Journal*, p. A14.

Hargreaves, A. (2009). The fourth way of change: Towards an age of inspiration and sustainability. In A. Hargreaves & M. Fullan (Eds.), *Change wars*. Bloomington, IN: Solution Tree.

Hargreaves, A., & Fink, D. (2006). Depth: Learning and integrity. In A. Hargreaves & D. Fink, *Sustainable leadership* (pp. 23–54). San Francisco: Jossey-Bass.

Leithwood, K. (2001). School leadership in the context of accountability. *International Journal of Leadership in Education, 4*(3), 217–235.

Looker, E. D., & Thiessen, V. (2003). *The digital divide in Canadian schools: Factors affecting student access to and use of information technology.* Retrieved March 7, 2009, from http://www. statcan.gc.ca/pub/81-597-x/81-597-x2003001-eng.pdf

Lorenzo, G. & Ittelson, J. (2005). *An overview of e-portfolios.* Retrieved March 7, 2009, from http://net.educause.edu/ir/library/pdf/ELI3001.pdf

Linn, R. L. (2003). Accountability: Responsibility and reasonable expectations. *Educational Researcher, 32*(7), 3–13.

McEwen, N. (2006). *The impact of educational accountability in Alberta since 1995.* Paper presented at the Canadian Society for the Study of Education annual conference, Toronto, ON.

Mupinga, D. (2005). Distance education in high schools: Benefits, challenges, and suggestions. *Clearing House, 78*(3), 105–108. Retrieved from the Academic Search Complete database.

O'Dwyer, L., Carey, R., & Kleiman, G. (2007). A study of the effectiveness of the Louisiana Algebra I online course. *Journal of Research on Technology in Education, 39*(3), 289–306. Retrieved from the Academic Search Complete database.

Ranson, S. (2003). Public accountability in the age of neo-liberal governance. *Journal of Education Policy, 18*(5), 459–480. Retrieved from the Academic Search Complete database.

Sahlberg, P. (2007). Education policies for raising student learning: The Finnish approach. *Journal of Education Policy, 22*(2), 147–171. Retrieved from the Academic Search Complete database.

Sahlberg, P. (2008). *From periphery to limelight: Educational change in Finland.* Unpublished manuscript.

Stitzlein, S. M., Feinberg, W., Greene, J., & Miron, L. (2007). Illinois project for democratic accountability. *Educational Studies: Journal of the American Educational Studies Association, 42*(2), 139–155. doi: 10.1080/00131940701513235.

Whitty, G., Power, S., & Halpin, D. (1998). *Devolution and choice in education: The school, the state and the market.* Buckingham, England: Open University Press.

7. LITERACY, ACCOUNTABILITY AND INCLUSIVE EDUCATION

Possibilities for Re-framing Alberta's Literacy Framework

Alberta's public education system serves increasingly diverse populations and, in many schools, the pressure of attending to the individual literacy needs of students while, at the same time, covering an extensive, state-mandated curriculum has become extremely challenging for teachers (Alberta Teachers' Association [ATA], 2008; Couture & Liying, 2000). This is especially so given the province's large-scale, standardized testing program and the high-stakes associated with the publication of test results. Our combined experiences (including roles as classroom teachers, reading specialist, literacy coordinator, humanities curriculum leader, school administrator and literacy policy researcher) have taught us that, despite the fact that the standardized tests do not account for many of the crucial processes and tacit dimensions of student learning and literacy development, when test scores are low, the pressure to improve results is felt at the classroom, school and district levels. One of the unintended consequences of this is that teaching and learning become shaped by a focus on what is necessary to improve test scores, often at the expense of the authentic and meaningful experiences that students need to successfully develop the literacies necessary for participating in and contributing to a democratic society. This chapter stems from our common interest in the local and lived experiences of teachers and school leaders as they attempt to meet the expectations for successful literacy learning and teaching in a context in which the process-oriented goals of literacy curriculum and the results-oriented goals of accountability systems are often at odds and difficult to reconcile. In addition to this interest, it is our common desire to learn more about the relationships among literacy, accountability and inclusive education.

In this chapter, we examine a specific pair of policy texts: *Literacy, More than Words: Summary of Input on a Literacy Framework for Alberta* (Alberta Advanced Education and Technology [AAET], 2008) and the draft of *A Literacy Framework for Alberta* (Alberta Education, 2008b). Using the approaches of critical policy sociology (Ball, 1997; 1994), we focus on how statements in these documents about literacy and accountability "values" and "outcomes" intersect and work intertextually to produce certain conceptions and priorities not only for literacy, but for accountability for literacy education. Thus, although these policy documents cover a range of issues and considerations, we focus specifically on what is articulated about accountability and students' literacy needs and learning, with an

K.D. Gariepy, B.L. Spencer and J.-C. Couture (eds.), Educational Accountability:
Professional Voices From the Field, 79–93.

additional interest in how literacy and accountability are to address issues of diversity and inclusion. We suggest that the difficulty educators experience in attempting to simultaneously meet the expectations of policies for both literacy and accountability is rooted in texts such as these framework documents. We identify alignment as a key policy effect and we examine how certain discourses operate to produce the framework recommendations for shared responsibility and accountability and for standardization and coherence. We contend that these discourses, along with policy alignment, promote "external coherence" and "top-down" accountability, which are at cross-purposes with the documents' other recommendations for process-oriented approaches to literacy education. In order to makes sense of the tension, we draw on literature that presents some of the critiques of externally driven, results-oriented approaches to literacy learning, teaching and assessment. We conclude by offering some suggestions for "internal coherence" and "holistic accountability" that might serve as alternative ideas for how literacy and accountability are presently being conceptualized in the *Literacy Framework* draft. It is our hope that this work may inform the "next steps" of the framework initiative and the development of subsequent policies.

We would like to be clear that our critique is not meant to dismiss the input of the forum participants and the hard work that has gone into the development of the draft of the *Literacy Framework*; rather, we hope that by drawing attention to the limits of the framework process, recommendations and potential policy implications, we can open some space for thinking about how accountability for literacy could be framed differently and, therefore, enacted in a way that "puts real learning first" (ATA, 2008).

RECENT CONSULTATION AND A FRAMEWORK FOR LITERACY IN ALBERTA

In order to participate in the pan-Canadian dialogue on literacy led by the Council of Ministers of Education, Canada, the Alberta Ministry of Advanced Education and Technology (2008) held the Alberta Literacy Forum in the spring of 2008. The Forum brought together 539 participants from various sectors to contribute to the discussion and to identify "what was important to improve literacy policy, programs and services in Alberta" (p. 2). The product of the forum was the document, *Literacy, More than Words: Summary of Input on a Literacy Framework for Alberta* (AAET, 2008), which summarizes the responses and recommendations for action.

At the forum, participants were provided with a *Forum Workbook*. This included background information on the provincial literacy context, the Alberta Government's position on literacy education and the rationale for a literacy framework for all levels of education in Alberta. It also included "a proposed definition, vision, values and outcomes to guide literacy in Alberta" (AAET, 2008, p. 3) and, for each of these topics, questions that were used to elicit responses during small-group table discussions.

The definition of literacy that was provided in the *Workbook* as a potential definition for the framework is as follows:

Literacy is not simply the ability to read and write but is the full range of competencies that allow individuals to think critically, communicate effectively and solve problems in a variety of contexts to achieve their personal goals, develop their knowledge and potential and participate fully in society. The development and retention of literacy competencies is also life long.

A comprehensive literacy framework recognizes the early experiences at home that contribute to oral language and literacy development, the foundational competencies for literacy built through the K-12 system and the need for adults to have opportunities to develop and build on their foundational literacy competencies. (AAET, 2008, p. 4)

The potential vision statement presented was: "All people in Alberta have opportunities to develop and expand their literacy competencies to participate fully and successfully in living, learning, and work" (p. 4). The *Workbook* also included a set of potential value statements:
Literacy policies, programs and services:
– are based on shared responsibility and accountability,
– acknowledge and value cultures, strengths, abilities and needs of individuals,
– support innovation and excellence in teaching and learning,
– are developed and implemented through open, honest, consistent and
– transparent processes. (AAET, 2008, p. 5)
The following possible outcomes for a literacy framework were provided:
As a province, we are working towards:
– programs and services that are inclusive and accessible to all Albertans,
– all individuals developing and enhancing their literacy competencies,
– education and training providers delivering quality literacy programs and services,
– literacy development supported and sustained through partnerships, and
– policies, programs and services that are designed to provide a continuum of literacy development. (AAET, 2008, p. 6)
The participants' comments in response to the possible definition, vision, values and outcomes, and the associated questions for each, constitute the input summarized in the *Literacy: More than Words* document. For the purposes of this analysis, we focus on the input generated for the possible outcomes for a literacy framework because they relate specifically to how notions of literacy are connected to understandings of accountability. This input, some of which was also identified as "key challenges to and solutions for improving literacy in Alberta" (AAET, 2008, p. 7), was organized into four themes. The first, *public awareness of literacy*, summarizes significant literacy issues and focuses on the value of literacy to society. The second, *resources*, points to the importance of an integrated and continuous program of literacy learning, especially as this relates to supports for students who struggle, and the provision of adequate resources to ensure access to literacy programs and excellence in teaching and delivery. The third theme, one on

which we want to focus, is *evaluation, measurability and accountability*. It is itemized as follows:

- Concrete goals with specific targets, timelines and common measures (qualitative and quantitative) are required to evaluate whether literacy is improving over time.
- There needs to be accountability – a discussion around what success means, how it is measured, and what happens with learners and programs when there is a lack of success.
- Government leadership was seen as necessary along with a requirement for annual reporting on progress. (AAET, 2008, p. 6)

The fourth theme, cultural diversity, another area of particular interest to us, outlines the importance of considering the views of different cultural groups and of respecting and integrating diverse worldviews and values into policies and programs for literacy learning.

Reflecting many of the same responses to the prompts and questions about possible outcomes, the document also includes participant input about "barriers and solutions." This is organized according to the following themes: *raising awareness, resources, coordination and partnerships, qualified instructors and volunteers* and *common definitions and standards*. Here, with our interest in accountability, we focus on the challenges and solutions related to common definitions and standards. These are outlined in the document as follows:

- Government leadership [is] key to ... having a continuum of learning reflected at the provincial level. Ministries and programs need to work together towards common goals, share information and opportunities. This would reduce duplication and overlap, create a more purposeful approach and link expertise and resources.
- Additionally, establishing benchmarks for literacy would allow for a common assessment process and feed the development of curriculum and lesson plans for use in a wide array of contexts.
- Improved assessment would assist in long-term planning, increasing account-ability and creating more options for learners. (AAET, 2008, p. 10)

A more comprehensive list of solutions appears in an appendix. These solutions are related to: responding to the diverse circumstances and needs of individual learners, with specific reference to immigrant populations; ensuring high standards for teachers, instructors and coordinators and the resources to support these groups (e.g., adequate compensation and professional development); and providing access to relevant resources and technologies. Under the heading "Standards in Learner Assessment and Program Evaluation," the following solutions are listed:

- ... a provincial commitment to work towards a certain benchmarked level of literacy skills would create consistency.
- .... common measures and standards of achievement so that learning is measureable and students can more easily transfer from opportunity to opportunity, knowing they operate with the same benchmarks....
- Common assessment processes and tools would assist with long-term planning and help measure literacy outcomes.

– Ongoing research is crucial to literacy in defining best practices, understanding what is happening in the Canadian and international context and building proactive responses to changes in the social environment. (AAET, 2008, p. 19)

The document concludes by stating that "there was consensus among the 539 participants on the key components of what should be included in a literacy framework for Alberta and the solutions for improving literacy for all ages" (p. 11). Key recommendations were listed as follows:

– Policies, programs and services need to be learner-centred, respectful and responsive to cultural differences.
– Resources are needed to expand programs and services, to hire and retain qualified staff and provide professional development to ensure that they remained qualified.
– Accountability was stressed with the need for an overall literacy plan with clear roles and responsibilities, common literacy benchmarks and assessment tools, defined targets, measures and timelines with regular reporting on progress. (AAET, 2008, p. 11)

These key action recommendations were incorporated into the May 2008 draft of *A Literacy Framework for Alberta* (Alberta Education, 2008b), which is to provide the framework for future literacy policies and program directions for the "current K-12, advanced education and workforce development systems" (AAET, 2008, p. 14).

The draft of the Framework includes the following "values:"

Literacy policies, programs and services:

– Are learner-centred and responsive to the strengths, abilities and needs of individuals.
– Acknowledge and value the language, culture, spirituality and traditions of learners, families and communities.
– Are delivered through collaborative partnerships.
– Support innovation and excellence in teaching and learning.
– Are based on shared responsibility and accountability.
– Are developed and implemented through open, honest, consistent and transparent processes. (Alberta Education, 2008b, p. 5)

The following "outcomes" are also included:

– Programs and services are inclusive and accessible to all learners.
– Individuals develop and enhance their literacy competencies.
– Education and training providers have the capacity and the infrastructure to deliver quality literacy programs and services.
– Collaborative partnerships support and sustain literacy programs and services.
– Policies, programs and services support a continuum of literacy development for Albertans of all ages. (p. 5)

Some "possible strategies" related to the accountability-focused forum recommendations are as follows:

– Develop, evaluate and share standardized curricula, lesson plans and teaching strategies.
– Conduct research on the development and identification of benchmarks for quality programs and services.

- Align foundational curricula and programs across the range of learning and training providers, early learning, K-12 and adult.
- Provide provincial leadership through a cross-ministry mechanism to coordinate literacy policies, programs and service ...
- Create definitions for a literacy continuum, benchmarks and standardized assessment tools that are linked to international adult literacy measures.
- Develop a plan with specific targets, timelines and common measures and report annually on the progress. (p. 6)

FRAMING THE FRAMEWORK: POLICY ALIGNMENT

We argue that together, the process and the texts of the Alberta Literacy Forum is an example of policy *alignment*. Alignment refers to the organization and assembly of policies and practices according to purpose, across time and space. Through policy alignment, a range of texts, strategies and projects are linked and integrated so that their arguments and promises appear as shared knowledge and commonly accepted ideas. Alignment rationalizes and perpetuates policy values and objectives (Miller, 1990).

To begin, policy alignment is a result of process. Assumed to have democratizing effects, public and partnership consultations such as the Forum have increasingly become a feature of educational policy development processes. However, while consultative discussions do generate broad-based input, policymaking, in whatever form, is fundamentally political (Ball, 1994). Representation of diverse interests does not eliminate the subtle and complex ways in which power relations are at play (Bowe, Ball, & Gold, 1992; Fairclough, 1992). Thus, attention must be paid to how authority and framing work together to assert particular perspectives and positions. Specifically, those who have the authority to invite participants and to frame the parameters for input are, to varying degrees, also directing and regulating who is involved and, therefore, who has voice and influence; what can and cannot be said; and, ultimately, what is and is not included in the policies that are the product of the consultation. This, we argue, is exemplified in some of the discursive processes of the Alberta Literacy Forum, especially since these ultimately produced texts. For example, the report begins by stating that the Minister of Education, in his welcoming address at the Forum, "challenged stakeholders to take a look at Alberta's view, vision and values, as well as what the province is working towards, and to provide insight to shape the direction of literacy in this province" (AAET, 2008, p. 2). It is clear that the view, vision and values Henke spoke of were defined prior to the forum and were included as the key points of focus in the *Forum Workbook*. Further, we contend that, while participants were asked to respond and offer suggestions to improve the "potential" or "possible" definition, vision, values and outcomes that were presented in the *Workbook*, responses were contained and limited by the already established set of discussion questions that accompanied the definition, vision, values and outcomes.

Particular to our interests in how conceptions of literacy and accountability intersect in the framework documents, we argue that, while the forum participants did offer critiques and supplementary ideas through the consultation, the findings reported in key theme areas were compiled from the input framed by the pre-determined focus and the deliberate process established by the *Workbook*. To review, possible value statements included the concepts of individual cultures, abilities and needs, support for innovation and excellence in teaching and learning, shared responsibility and accountability and consistent and transparent processes. Possible framework outcomes included the concepts of inclusivity, accessibility, quality, a continuum of literacy development, partnerships and development of individuals' competencies (AAET, 2008, pp. 5–6). Thus, it is not surprising that the conceptions of literacy education related to diversity, accessibility and inclusivity reflect and align with the statements related to values and outcomes promoted in other literacy policies and documents for K-12 education in Alberta. Among these are the *K-3 Numeracy/Literacy Report* (Alberta Education, 2006a), *Supporting the Literacy Learner: Promising Literacy Strategies in Alberta* (Alberta Education, 2008c), and the various *Programs of Study* (i.e., curricula, which emphasize literacy across disciplines). It is also not surprising that the focus of the *Forum Workbook* on quality, excellence and conceptions of accountability that emphasize cross-level coherence, consistency, transparency and competencies reflect and align with those already defined and at work in Alberta's broader accountability policies, including the *Renewed Framework for Funding School Jurisdictions* (Alberta Education, 2006b) and the *Accountability Pillar* (Alberta Education, 2009). In this sense, the *Summary* and *Framework* documents operate as a medium of and for policy alignment. Their unified and consistent representations, arguments and recommendations are textually mediated within a broader knowledge complex wherein the discourses of literacy and accountability are assembled by and reproduce certain conceptions about education and reform (Ball, 1994; Dean, 1999; Rose, 1999). Thus, their function as particularly useful textual products also makes them authoritative sources of intertextual knowledge production (Foucault, 1972).[i] That is, policy documents are shaped by and shape the discourses of broader state policy aspirations and agendas. We return to this argument later in the chapter.

As Rose (1999) explains, such policy alignment is a primary goal of governments. Given this, we can see why the forum was organized in relation to existing policy definitions, visions and values. However, while often seen as "the way it is," such effects should not be taken for granted. Where alignment functions to organize participant input and to produce text that reaffirms existing conceptions, values and objectives, its product should be scrutinized; the assumptions upon which policy claims and recommendations are predicated should be examined. Thus, in the following section, we analyze the discourse of the Framework to make explicit what is assumed about the relationships among literacy education, accountability, and diversity and inclusion in order to reveal how and why, in practice, these assumptions are at the root of contention and difficulty.

INPUT THEMES AND RECOMMENDATIONS:COHERENCE
AND STANDARDIZATION

The accountability recommendations of the *Literacy, More than Words* and the *Literacy Framework* are full of language that defines literacy as a complex notion, "extending beyond reading and writing to extracting and critically analyzing information to solve problems in different situations" (Alberta Education, 2008b, p. 4). The discourse describing the proposed literacy programs includes words such as learner-centered and responsive, and statements about the value of individual abilities and needs and of cultural and community sensitivity. Outcomes and proposed strategies include the language of inclusiveness, accessibility and alternate delivery, and of recognizing and valuing informal learning. At the same time, the vision is for "a coordinated comprehensive approach" (Alberta Education, 2008b, p. 5) to literacy development. In this regard, repeated is the language of consistency, continuation, cross-ministry provision (from early children to adult education), formalized partnerships for coordinated and sustained programs and "learner pathways" for transferability between programs on a "literacy continuum." It is important to note that, in these terms, the discourse of coherence is also the discourse of shared responsibility, another focus of the *Framework* document. Moreover, by appearing in the same value statement, the meaning of shared responsibility and of accountability becomes blurred.

As an effect, the discourse of standardization is not only about shared responsibility for program coherence, it is also about shared responsibility in the terms proposed for accountability outcomes, such as: align foundational curriculum; define competencies and essential skills; identify and incorporate "effective" practices; credential practitioners; develop, evaluate and share standardized curricula, lesson plans and teaching strategies; standardize learning outcomes, assessment and reporting; align and link literacy measures; create definitions, benchmarks and standardized assessment tools; and "develop a plan with specific target timelines and common measures and report annually on the progress" (Alberta Education, 2008, p. 6). Through such articulations, we argue, it is in the discourse of shared responsibility and standardization that the language of program coherence becomes intermeshed with the language of results-oriented accountability. Specifically, the discourses of shared responsibility and standardization that emphasize consistence, coordination and coherence become synonymous with the discourses of shared responsibility and standardization that emphasize results-oriented accountability.

In policy documents, the language, meaning and the structures we use for definitions, visions, values, outcomes and strategies may appear to be quite straightforward; however, this is not always the case. Through discourse, texts produce knowledge and mediate practice (Ball, 1994; Fairclough, 1992). In the above analysis, we can see how the discourses of the *Literacy Framework for Alberta* assert certain assumptions and understandings about literacy education and accountability. Specifically, through these policy articulations, shared responsibility and accountability are conflated in the language of standardization for coherence. We argue that, in the text, they are used in a way that has them fit together quite naturally and, indeed, convincingly. As a result, what the policy assumes and establishes about the relationship among ideas of shared responsibility, accountability, standardization and coherence is presented as "consensus" and is accepted without consideration of the contradictions inherent in such conceptualizations and of the implications of putting such ideas into practice.

The emphasis on and combination of discourses such as these is not unusual in Canada's "hybrid" education policy frameworks, which are often attempts by governments to respond to myriad internal and external challenges and pressures for change (Ben Jaafar &Anderson, 2007). However, it is in practice—in attempts to implement policy—that the contradictions among these ideas are revealed. The tension lies in the coupling and confusion of the discourses related to what Ben Jaafar and Anderson refer to as a results-oriented accountability approach and process-oriented operational features. We argue that it is precisely in this tension that educators find themselves. In the following section, we draw on current literature and research that describes the challenges and effects of the tensions of implementing results-oriented accountability approaches for process-oriented literacy education.

EXTERNAL COHERENCE AND TOP-DOWN ACCOUNTABILITY: CRITIQUES OF STANDARDIZED CURRICULUM AND TESTING FOR LITERACY DEVELOPMENT

We argue that the unintended policy consequences described above can be considered effects of what Honig and Hatch (2004) call *external policy coherence*. This kind of "coherence from the outside in" (p. 17) is characterized by the top-down "systemic and standards-based reform initiatives of the 1980s and 1990s [which] treated policy incoherence as a problem of policy design" (p. 17). Resulting were policies based on the "assumptions that external ... alignment of standards, curricula, and assessments by states and districts could ... focus schools on specific, challenging academic content and performance standards and a vision that all students can learn" (p. 17). According to Honig and Hatch, research reveals that such reform initiatives were fraught with problems. For example, such policies were designed on the basis of a "'systemic reform fallacy' – the belief that the multitude of external reform demands 'can be handled at the point of policy formation by creating conglomerate policies that subsume the different strands of reform activity into one carefully-orchestrated whole' (Knapp et al., 1998, p. 416)" (p. 17). The reality is that, "in schools, political values of democratic governance and participation, inclusiveness, and local determinism complicate attempts to streamline goals and strategies from the outside in" (p. 17). This is evidenced in current literature and research that shows how attempts to standardize literacy education thwart the very values and curriculum objectives for inclusion and opportunity that are the imperatives upon which literacy policies rest.

For instance, scholars argue that curriculum coherence has the tendency to focus and narrow objectives and to impose constraints on what can be taught and when. Lemke (2007) points to the "dysfunction" built into the structure of contemporary schooling as a result of standardization. Specific to literacy education and student learning, content and time constraints imposed by standardized curricula limit the potential for students to pursue their individual interests, to learn at their own pace and to develop deep understanding and critical perspectives, especially when this requires prolonged teacher support or project-based learning. Furthermore, when a key feature of curriculum coherence is accountability, standardized testing becomes a preoccupation. Higgins, Miller and Wegmann (2007) argue that the principles and practices of appropriate literacy assessment have been eroded by high-stakes testing, which is "not about student learning" (p. 310). Bainbridge and Malicky (2000) point out that standardized tests fail to attend to the social constructivist conceptions of learning that are essential to literacy development: critical thinking, construction of meaning and collaborative learning. This has a narrowing effect on curriculum and teaching because it is often the case that "what is taught is determined by what is tested" (p. 116). Because literacy development is difficult to assess through standardized tests, the narrowing effect is exacerbated when conceptions of literacy become limited to reading and writing (Gee, 2003). As Afflerbach (2005) argues, standardized reading tests come with a set of "liabilities:" they may be detrimental to student motivation, disrupt high quality teaching and learning, take away resources (i.e., time and money) that could be used in the classroom, and generate data that are increasingly misused, which can result in the negative labeling of students who are in early stages of literacy development.

External coherence also undermines the professional knowledge and experience of teachers and ignores the importance of local determinism. As Allington and Cunningham (2007) contend, the movement to standardize curriculum results in a narrow conception of literacy that does not acknowledge that the professional teacher is in the best position to understand the literacy skills and needs of students. Maruatona (2002) agrees, arguing that decisions about curriculum and pedagogy should reside at the local level and that curricula should be diversified to reflect the specific needs of learners and the cultures of the school community. Similarly, for Mulcahy and Irwin (2008), student engagement is central to literacy learning. They suggest that "the teacher in the classroom should have the authority to engage students in a living curriculum that pertains to their daily lives. The community must determine what this curriculum is rather than ... government officials who lack local knowledge" (p. 201).

The above arguments help us to understand how the effects of program coherence (i.e., a narrowed and constrained standardized program for literacy teaching, learning and assessment) can also be in contraction to the democratic principles of participation and inclusiveness. For example, a coherent, standardized literacy curriculum may be detrimental to learners of diverse urban schools because a decrease in local control disconnects students from cultural and linguistic communities that are necessary for educational success (Kuchapski, 1998). Specific to top-down accountability approaches, Berlak (1999) contends that standardized tests are "an effort to put an end to the most valuable asset of a multicultural society: its vibrant cacophony of views about what constitutes truth, knowledge, and learning" (para. 6). Furthermore, as Gee (2003) argues, the standards-focused accountability agenda implies that if all students "are simply exposed to the same tests and facts in school, they will all 'pass the test' and problems of equity will thereby be taken care of' (p. 27). According to Gee, current research in literacy studies calls for a more sophisticated view of learning assessment and a more complicated view of equity. This research challenges the ways in which standardized testing has constructed the relationships among accountability, literacy and equity (Gee, 2003).

We wish to pick up on Gee's (2003) point above to return to our analysis of the *Literacy, More than Words* and the *A Literacy Framework for Alberta* documents. We suggest that the proposed literacy framework is a clear example of a "hybrid" policy initiative that demonstrates how the province's education ministries are attempting to respond to the broader goals and agendas of the current government and to increasing external pressures on public education. We have focused on two of these demands: accountability and literacy education. Through our analysis of the discourse and assumptions of the literacy framework texts, we have argued that through the language of coherence, standardization, shared responsibility and accountability, the tensions that are inherent in the implementation of results-oriented accountability approaches and process-oriented literacy education are obscured or glossed over. Specifically, as the literature suggests, in practice, educators and students bear the brunt of living the tension. While teachers struggle to meet the literacy needs of their students, they are held within a regime of standardization that hinders the achievement of broader, democratic goals of public education: access, inclusion and full participation for an equitable society. Paradoxically, while the discourses of inclusiveness and the value given to the abilities, needs and cultures of individuals and communities are a central feature of the framework documents, the discourses of shared responsibility and standardization, whether of program coherence or of accountability, dominate and, in practice, can undermine the very goals they are meant to achieve.

In effect, frameworks assuming that results-oriented accountability approaches *and* process-oriented literacy education can be practiced without difficulty are inherently problematic. Thus, we wonder about what the documents refer to as "next steps" and are particularly interested in how the provincial framework for literacy will shape Alberta Education's plans for literacy development in the K-12 system. We are heartened by some of the definitions, guiding principles and strategies outlined in the November, 2008 draft of the *K–12 Literacy Discussion Paper* (Alberta Education, 2008a). Many of these reflect and extend those of the framework documents. For example, the *Discussion Paper* attends to the values of access, inclusion and participation and reflects the research about curriculum and pedagogy that supports such values. A specific example is that authentic assessment is featured in the document's section on evaluation and assessment.

However, based on the same concerns about policy alignment, intertextuality and the operation of discourse outlined in our analysis of the *Literacy, More than Words* and the *Literacy Framework* documents, we are also troubled by the *K–12 Literacy Discussion Paper*. That is, the mention of authentic assessment in the *Discussion Paper* is preceded by the following statement:

Trends identified through provincial assessment results will help inform the priority actions for literacy. Alberta Education will use current assessments; e.g., the various Provincial Achievement Test results combined with student, parent and community surveys and high school completion rates, to measure the success of the priority actions on literacy. (Alberta Education, 2008a, p. 11)

While the above passage seems to indicate some recognition of the limits of large-scale standardized assessments, considering what the literature says about the appropriateness of such measures for evaluating literacy curriculum, teaching, and learning, we have concerns about this accountability statement. Moreover, in light of our arguments about the power of policy documents to produce and to reassert priorities and recommendations based on certain assumptions, we wonder about the potential of a K-12 literacy program that may be designed on problematic assumptions of results-oriented accountability approaches *and* process-oriented literacy education that, in practice, are the root of tensions, difficulty and frustration at the classroom level.

CONCLUDING REMARKS:
HOLISTIC AND AUTHENTIC ACCOUNTABILITY FOR CRAFTED COHERENCE

To conclude, we would like to offer some suggestions for re-framing the proposed framework by incorporating ideas about accountability that may be more conducive to achieving the goals of a robust literacy program for all students. We draw on Reeves's (2002) arguments for holistic accountability, the guidelines for authentic accountability proposed by the National Center for Fair and Open Testing (2004) and Honig and Hatch's (2004) suggestions for "crafted" coherence.

To begin, Reeves (2002) defines holistic accountability as follows:

Holistic accountability is … a continuous cycle in which research informs professional practice and professional practice yields evidence of its impact on student achievement. Based on this evidence, leaders and policymakers can make informed decisions and rationally allocate resources. These resources, in turn, support more effective research, professional practice, and leadership. (p. 19)

In this model, the position and practice of the professional educator is central. Evidence of student achievement is gathered through practice, at the classroom and school levels. Thus, teachers, leaders and policymakers "receive much more information than a set of test scores; they gain insight into the antecedents of excellence" (p. 20) – those indicators "that *practitioners* [italics added] believe are related to student achievement" (p. 19). As Reeves warns, when accountability is characterized by "a litany of test scores, teachers will never have productive discussions of accountability data" (p. 28). For example, large-scale, standardized test scores may have their place (i.e., as benchmark data and one small piece of evidence), but Reeves argues that their use in traditional, results-oriented accountability systems has missed a significant link: more important than standardized test results "is evidence of what happened before the score was calculated" (p. 21).

The National Center for Fair and Open Testing (2004) principles for authentic accountability echo Reeves' (2004) ideas, also arguing for the use of "helpful indicators" that take into consideration multiple forms of evidence and do not rely on data generated through externally mandated, results-based accountability models. "Helpful" student assessment is explained as follows: "Skilled use of feedback to students is one of the most powerful means teachers have for improving learning. Most assessment must be classroom-based and used by well-prepared teachers." The authority of an authentic accountability system originates at the local school and community levels and the role of higher levels of government is to

> ensure adequate provision and fair use of resources so as to provide equity of opportunities; safeguard civil and human rights; disseminate knowledge; provide focused help where needed; and intervene in localities only when necessary and with methods that have been shown to be successful.

Reflecting these accountability guidelines are Honig and Hatch's (2004) suggestions for crafted coherence, which put emphasis on "inside out" accountability rather than "outside in," externally-driven approaches. This involves new relationships where "schools become central decision makers and school district central offices become supporters of others' decisions and both face demands to work together in new ways" (p. 28).

We contend that the above suggestions for holistic and authentic accountability approaches that shift the locus of authority and control from the outside to the inside and recognize that coherence cannot be effectively mandated through top-down accountability policies are appropriate considerations for the development of a literacy framework in Alberta. By putting into perspective how the discourses of standardized, results-oriented policies for accountability obscure and undermine the objectives of literacy education, we hope to interrupt the ways in which our current accountability policies perpetuate the contradictions and tensions that are not only frustrating the efforts of educators but are also undermining the possibilities of a successful literacy program. In addition, by pointing to approaches that emphasize internal coherence rather that external coherence, we hope to open space to imagine accountability for literacy as being process-oriented rather than results-oriented. Thus, we want to direct attention to and endorse those aspects of *A Literacy Framework for Alberta* and the *K–12 Literacy Discussion Paper* that are specific to a program that will emphasize and promote participation, inclusion and equity and that will best serve all of Alberta's students.

NOTES

[1] Foucault (1972) stressed that texts exist only in relation to others: Any single text "is caught up in a system of references to other books, other texts, other sentences: it is a node within a network.... Its unity is variable and relative ... [within] a complex field of discourse" (p. 23).

REFERENCES

Afflerbach, P. (2005). National reading conference policy brief: High stakes testing and reading assessment. *Journal of Literacy Research, 37*(2), 151–162.

Alberta Advanced Education and Technology. (2008). *Literacy, more than words: Summary of input on a literacy framework for Alberta*. Retrieved February 1, 2009, from http://www.advancededucation. gov.ab.ca/other/literacy/Summary_of_Literacy_Forum_Input.pdf

Alberta Education. (2006a). *K-3 numeracy/literacy report*. Retrieved February 1, 2009, from http://education.alberta.ca/media/354803/k-3_numeracy_literacy_report-2006.pdf

Alberta Education. (2006b). Renewed framework for funding school jurisdictions. In Alberta Education, *2006-2007 funding manual for school authorities*. Retrieved February 2, 2009, from http://education.alberta.ca/media/482898/framework.pdf

Alberta Education. (2008a). *K–12 literacy discussion paper, November 2008 draft*. Retrieved February 2, 2009, from http://education.alberta.ca/apps/literacy/Default.asp

Alberta Education. (2008b). *A literacy framework for Alberta: Draft*. Retrieved February 2, 2009, from http://education.alberta.ca/literacy/docs/Literacy_Framework_Draft.pdf

Alberta Education. (2008c). *Supporting the literacy learner: Promising literacy strategies in Alberta*. Retrieved February 1, 2009, from http://education.alberta.ca/media/696711/support.pdf

Alberta Education. (2009). *Accountability pillar*. Retrieved February 15, 2009, from http://education. alberta.ca/admin/funding/accountability.aspx

Alberta Teachers' Association. (2008). *Real learning first: The teaching profession's view of student assessment, evaluation and accountability*. Retrieved February 2, 2009, from http://www.teachers.ab.ca/ Issues%20In%20Education/Real%20Learning%20First/Pages/Teachers%20put%20Real%20Learni ng%20First.aspx

Allington, R. L., & Cunningham, P. M. (2007). *Schools that work: Where all children read and write*. Boston: Pearson/Allyn & Bacon.

Bainbridge, J., & Malicky, G. (with Payne, P). (2000). *Constructing meaning: Balancing elementary language arts* (2nd ed.). Toronto: Harcourt Canada.

Ball, S. J. (1994). *Education reform: A critical post-structural approach*. Buckingham, England: Open University Press.

Ball, S. J. (1997). Policy sociology and critical social research: A personal review of recent education policy and policy research. *British Journal of Educational Studies, 23*(3), 257–274.

Ben Jaafar, S., & Anderson, S. (2007). Policy trends and tensions in accountability for educational management and services in Canada. *Alberta Journal of Educational Research, 53*(2), 207–227.

Berlak, H. (1999). Standards and the control of knowledge. *Rethinking Schools Online, 13*(3). Retrieved February 2, 2009, from http://www.rethinkingschools.org/archive/13_03/control.shtml

Bowe, R., Ball, S. J., & Gold, A. (1992). *Reforming education and changing schools: Case studies in policy sociology*. London: Routledge.

Couture, J. C., & Liying, C. (2000). Teachers' work in the global culture of performance. *Alberta Journal of Educational Research, 46*(1), 65.

Dean, M. (1999). *Governmentality: Power and rule in modern society*. London: Sage.

Fairclough, N. (1992). *Discourse and social change*. Cambridge, England: Polity Press.

Foucault, M. (1972). *The archaeology of knowledge and the discourse on language*. New York: Pantheon.

Gee, J. P. (2003). The opportunity to learn: A language-based perspective on assessment. *Assessment in Education: Principles, Policy and Practice, 10*(1), 27–46.

Higgins, B., Miller, M., & Wegmann, S. (2007). Teaching to the test ... not! Balancing best practice and testing requirements in writing. *Reading Teacher, 60*(4), 310–319.

Honig, M. I., & Hatch, T. C. (2004). Crafting coherence: How schools strategically manage multiple, external demands. *Educational Researcher, 33*(8), 16–30.

Kuchapski, R. (1998). Accountability and the social good: Using Manzer's liberal framework in Canada. *Education and Urban Society, 301*(4), 531–545.

Lemke, J. (2007). Re-engineering education in America. *Language Arts, 85*(1), 52–60.

Maruatona, T. (2002). A critique of centralized curricula in literacy programs: The case of Botswana. *Journal of Adolescent and Adult Literacy, 45*(8), 736–745.

Miller, P. (1990). On the interrelations between accounting and the state. *Accounting Organizations and Society, 15*(4), 315–338.

Mulcahy, D. E., & Irwin, J. (2008). The standardized curriculum and delocalization: Obstacles to critical pedagogy. *Radical History Review*, 102, 201–213. doi: 10.1215/01636545-2008-024.

National Center for Fair and Open Testing. (2004). Draft principles for authentic accountability. *Fair Test*. Retrieved February 2, 2009, from http://www.fairtest.org/draft-principles-authentic-accountability

Reeves, D. B. (2002). *Hoistic accountability: Serving students, schools, and community*. Thousand Oaks, CA: Corwin Press.

Rose, N. (1999). *Powers of freedom: Reframing political thought*. Cambridge, England: Cambridge University Press.

RANDY HETHERINGTON

8. THE SUPERINTENDENCY

Building Cultures of Trust Through "Intelligent Accountability"

Many educational concepts, including the notion of "accountability," have multiple meanings based on their context or on the social and political forces that shape their meaning (Ben Jafaar & Anderson, 2007; Kuchapski, 1998). This in and of itself is not a problem until stakeholders begin a dialogue about accountability that involves varying interpretations. Considering the range of stakeholder relationships that are at play in complex educational systems (P. McRae, personal communication, April 18, 2008) the implications related to voicing, debating and understanding differing points of view can affect the level of trust that exists among the parties involved. Sahlberg (2007) states a need for a new type of mutual accountability in education that builds on professional responsibility and trust. He refers to this as "intelligent accountability" – a kind of accountability that promises to support both the development of students and the public good.

In this chapter I argue that the superintendency is a uniquely positioned office through which cultures of trust can be built and intelligent accountability can be promoted in order to serve all stakeholders of Alberta's public K-12 education system. First, I make the case that a complex system of stakeholder relationships exists in public education. Second, I focus on three key relationships within the complex system and I briefly describe the lines of accountability within these arrangements. I argue that the superintendency is pivotal in facilitating and mediating the accountability relationships, in promoting trust and in influencing positive change within the education system. Third, I reflect on the "crisis of trust" that precipitated Alberta's education reforms of the 1990s, gave birth to current accountability policies and continues to haunt our system. I draw on literature related to intelligent accountability to offer some suggestions for restoring and building trust cultures that are necessary for ensuring the best possible education system for Alberta's children.

THE SUPERINTENDENCY DEFINED

For the purposes of my discussion, the superintendency is understood to be the office of the chief educational officer of a public school division as selected by publicly elected trustees and appointed by the Minister of Education for the province of Alberta (School Act, 2007). The selection of the superintendent by elected trustees and the requirement of appointment by the Crown is a critical point. That is, it is assumed that the electorate has confidence in the

K.D. Gariepy, B.L. Spencer and J.-C. Couture (eds.), Educational Accountability:
Professional Voices From the Field, 95–103.
© *2009 Sense Publishers. All rights reserved.*

superintendent's ability to provide appropriate leadership to differing education stakeholder groups even though the complexity of doing this may not be fully understood. In this sense, I argue that the role of the superintendency can be understood in terms of "servant leadership" (Crippen, 2005), where the leader's own agenda is subordinated to and in service of the needs of school personnel, parents and students in the system and the general public (Fullan, 2003).

The work of the superintendency is related to the inherently complex and challenging political, economic, and organizational dimensions of the office (Fleishman, 1990). Furthermore, the superintendency is centrally situated within network of the education system, which includes, at the provincial level, the government, the ministries of finance and education and their applicable branches (e.g., curriculum, special education) and, at the local level, elected trustees, parents and community members and certified, paraprofessional and contract staff. The limits of the superintendency in decision-making authority, scope of duties and responsibilities, and guiding policies are in part determined at the provincial level as outlined in the School Act's (2007) sections referencing the Board Authority. In addition, policies at the local level that stipulate boundaries of responsibility, administrative guidelines that further specify required actions and procedures, collective agreements with certificated staff, contractual arrangements with service providers, and educational agreements with federal agencies all contribute to defining the superintendent's boundaries of influence and authority.

THE COMPLEX SYSTEM

The link between the superintendency and the concept of accountability is stipulated in terms of the decision and the responsibility to act. This is explained by Leithwood and Earl (2000) in their discussion of who is expected to provide an account to whom within an education system. They attach responsibility not only to the acts one undertakes but also to the role or position one occupies. The role of serving stakeholders in the attainment of the best possible educational system therefore requires the superintendency to account to stakeholders for decisions made and actions taken (Murgatroyd & Henry, 2007) What, then, is the relationship between the superintendency and these stakeholders? To answer that question we must understand Alberta's complex public education system.

Public education in Alberta is a complex system given that it exists in an advanced society, consists of many components interacting at multiple layers of the organization at different times, and is composed of diverse stakeholders (Kaput, Bar-Yam, Jacobson, Jakobsson, Lemke, & Wilensky, 2005) Being successful in this complex system depends on the ability to form collaborative relationships based on trust in the established hierarchy (Sahlberg, 2007). The educational hierarchy in Alberta has existed in its current form for many years (Dibski, 1979) and the superintendency is centrally positioned within that structure. The hierarchy suggests levels of authority but not the many and varied relationships that exist between the levels (Elmore, 1979). The site administrator, parents, teachers, support staff and students together form the school level while the superintendency or board authority, inclusive of executive staff, and the Council of Alberta School Superintendents, represent the board level. The departments of the Deputy Minister and zone representatives are the appointed level of government and the Minister, as representative of both the Crown and the governing political party, represents the elected level of government at the top of the hierarchy. I argue that because accountability is essential to all the relationships that exist between and among constituents at all levels, a strong culture of trust is necessary.

In making this claim I am defining a culture of trust by extending Magolda's (2000) concept of harmonious relationship. I suggest that cultures of trust also include a refined understanding of the reliability, ability and strength of an individual or office, so regarded by those within the relationship, such that information is exchanged freely. Understanding that this culture may be founded on faulty assumptions about the legitimacy or scope of authority, the culture nonetheless exists and guides the discussions and interactions of parties in the system. The discussions and inter- actions between two or more people or groups define the relationships, and the culture of trust developed as a result is unique as it is formative in nature, constantly being redefined with each new interaction which, in turn, influences subsequent actions or debate (Krajewski & Trevino, 2004). I propose that three of these relationships, each dependent on a culture of trust, are central to the discussion of accountability in education and should be given special consideration.

The Board Authority and the Public

The board authority is an organizational body, led by a superintendent who represents public schools within a school division and is advised by and advises a democratically elected board of trustees (School Act, 2007). For my purposes here, the "public" is broadly defined as those who, through participation, financial contribution or other involvement serve, or are served, by the K-12 education system in Alberta. Officially represented in the hierarchy by their elected trustees, members of the public can influence the system at a variety of levels, making their role somewhat unique. Public accountability for decisions affecting K-12 education can be requested at the professional level of the individual teacher, the administrative level of the school principal, the management level of the superintendent's office, the representative level of the board of trustees or the political level through the office of the Minister. This multi-level access to accountability makes the relationship between the public and the school board equally tenuous as a foundation for a culture of trust considering that the priorities of each level may be distinctly different. The diverse nature of "the public" is also problematic as there is likely no commonly held assumptions or beliefs about authority between any two sub-groups that reside within the body considered to be the public. Relationships here are highly contextual and variant (Shariff, 2006). As an office through which the desires and concerns of the government, the ministry, and the board as well as the desires and the concerns of parents, the public, and school personnel are directed and mediated, the superintendency offers an important hub for communication, facilitation, mediation and, therefore, for building trust.

The Board Authority and Teachers

Teachers, as professionals, have a complex relationship with the board authority. As employees of the board they are accountable to the board for provision of service as well as serving as agents of the board while conducting school business. Teachers are accountable through the board to the ministry for transmission of prescribed curriculum, valid assessment for and of learning, as well as adherence to board policy and regulations regarding all aspects of a teaching and supervision of students. The board, it could be argued, is morally obliged to provide a reasoned and supportive policy framework in which teachers can do their work; however, only Ministry guidelines, which generally and specifically outline the role of school boards, exist to guide this practice (School Act, 2007). The role of the board authority, especially since the superintendent is the supervisor of teachers' professional conduct, poses a problem to building trust. Typically, in the situation of administrators, that supervisory role is direct and, in the situation of teachers, indirect, through the auspices of the site-based administrator. The opportunity for the superintendent to significantly impact the professional and personal life of teachers and teachers in administrative roles is a barrier to a trust relationship developing. Without any reciprocal accountability to teachers for the actions of the board or superintendent, the imbalance can manifest distrust or, at best, a guarded approach to interactions of any kind. Here, again, the superintendent is positioned to mediate concerns and alleviate tensions.

Teachers and the Public

Perhaps the most interesting relationship of all exists between teachers and the broadly defined public in that it is constructed in direct and indirect ways. A teacher or group of teachers within a school community may develop a solid rapport with parents and, through their day-to-day decisions and actions, create strong accountability relationships and a culture of trust in their community. King (personal communication, April 19, 2008) states that the best educational decisions are made collaboratively between local boards, local teachers and the communities they serve. However, like other professions, teachers are also subject to account-ability by association. For example, headlines that reflect poorly on teachers and schools can, in the minds of those we collectively call the "public," be cause for concern and distrust and can result in calls for more accountability. Repairing a culture of trust that the superintendent may have had no part in damaging is difficult, and being held accountable at some level for the actions of all teachers is daunting to say the least. As the board's representative, the superintendent is again centrally positioned to, at a minimum, advocate for their employee groups within the local arena, and provide public support for their efforts. This can go far in building trust within the community and among stakeholders.

TRUST AND INTELLIGENT ACCOUNTABILITY

If my arguments thus far have made the case that the office of the superintendency functions to mediate and facilitate relationships and, potentially, to build cultures of trust in Alberta's complex accountability arrangements, what may be preventing a more encompassing, system-wide culture of trust from developing? The current debate between educators, scholars and government over accountability measures in the province's K-12 education system certainly suggests that a cohesive culture of trust does not yet exist. For example, the present *accountability pillar* framework has caused concern among educators who feel the pressure of being accountable for what is publically reported– standardized achievement test and satisfaction survey results. Specifically, questions about whether such measures are an appropriate reflection of what happens in schools and how educators ought to be held accountable are being asked (King, 2007; Taylor, Shultz, & Wishart Leard, 2005). Teachers continue to feel that their professional expertise and autonomy are challenged by the powerful accountability policies, and teacher morale has suffered (ATA, 2006; Couture & Liying, 2000; Taylor et al., 2005). The tensions related to accountability have put strain on the various stakeholder relationships and, I argue, have been detrimental to the cultures of trust of those on which I have focused: the board and the public, the board and the teachers, and the teachers and the public. What, then, is missing? I argue that intelligent accountability might be one answer.

Applied with different emphases, the idea of "intelligent accountability" has been promoted in educational circles by scholars such as Fullan (2004) and Hopkins (2005), and it is being applied in various school systems in the UK with the purpose of bringing a balance of qualitative and quantitative evidence to accountability systems. However, it is important to note that the idea of "intelligent accountability" was forwarded earlier by Onora O'Neill (2002) in the BBC's Reith Lectures entitled *A Question of Trust*. O'Neill's insightful arguments on the connection between trust and accountability are noteworthy:

> The diagnosis of a crisis of trust may be obscure: we are not sure whether there is a crisis of trust. But we are all agreed about the remedy. It lies in prevention and sanctions. Government, institutions and professionals should be made more accountable. And in the last two decades, the quest for greater accountability has penetrated all our lives … reaching parts that supposedly less developed forms of accountability did not reach.

I argue that O'Neill's interpretation applies to education, especially as the reforms in many nations and in Alberta during the 1990s were, in large part, a response to a perception that public schools had failed and education was in crisis (Brown, Halsey, Lauder, & Wells, 1997). This charge came from politicians, the general public, businesses and corporations, parents, and the media (Barlow & Robertson, 1994). To a significant degree, the crisis was a crisis of trust and was a result of several widely held notions: the programs of the 1960s and 1970s' liberal welfare state had produced inefficient, top-heavy bureaucracies; educational standards and quality had declined and schools had failed to graduate a workforce equipped with the skills for a "new" global economy; teachers were guilty of "provider capture" of education and, because of their "special interest" control, could not be trusted to make professional judgements about educational quality (Apple, 1993; Barlow & Robertson, 1994; Marginson, 1993; Ranson, 2003).

While there has been much debate about whether or not the crisis was real, perceived or actually manufactured, it was a powerful motivator and a period of significant public education reform ensued (Whitty, Power & Halpin, 1998). As Levin (2001) asserts in relation to Canadian contexts, some stakeholder arguments "that education is in a state of crisis seem not to have been generally accepted, but remain a strong part of official rhetoric nonetheless" (p. 14). A primary thrust of the various reform agendas was accountability, which was seen as an appropriate policy solution for the problem of restoring public trust in public education (Ranson, 2003). The following is O'Neill's (2002) position on the results of the accountability solution:

> For those of us in the public sector the new accountability takes the form of detailed control. An unending stream of new legislation and regulation, memoranda and instructions, guidance and advice floods into public sector institutions.... The new accountability culture aims at ever more perfect administrative control of institutional and professional life.

Alberta's current accountability context reflects O'Neill's (2002) assessment of the new accountability culture. I argue that the stakeholder tensions I describe above are rooted in the aims of detailed control. Is it any wonder trust relationships between stakeholders are strained and among practitioners, policy developers and politicians are tenuous at best? I contend that cultures of trust are essential to sound accountability policy and practice in Alberta schools and I submit that the superintendent is best situated as both the catalyst and facilitator for restoring and building trust. To build trust, O'Neill calls for "real" accountability – intelligent accountability:

> .... Intelligent accountability, I suspect, requires more attention to good governance and fewer fantasies about total control. Good governance is possible only if institutions are allowed some margin for self-governance of a form appropriate to their particular tasks, within a framework of financial and other reporting. Such reporting, I believe, is not improved by being wholly standardized or relentlessly detailed, and since much that has to be accounted for is not easily measured it cannot be boiled down to a set of stock performance indicators. Those who are called to account should give an account of what they have done and of their successes or failures to others who have sufficient time and experience to assess the evidence and report on it. Real accountability provides substantive and knowledgeable independent judgement of an institution's or professional's work.

According to Cowie and Croxford (2007), intelligent accountability in public education implies: "trust in professionals; a focus on self-evaluation; appropriate measures that do not distort the purposes of schooling; and measures that encourage the fullest development of every pupil" (p. 1). Crooks (2003) has offered six criteria for intelligent accountability:

- preserves and enhances trust among the key participants in the accountability processes.
- involves participants in the process, offering them a strong sense of professional responsibility and initiative. This, of course, contributes to trust.....
- promote deep, high quality learning in the domain to be assessed: the sort of learning that should have long-term payoff on any appropriate outcome measure. Deep learning takes time and focus, and is undermined by overemphasis on short-term goals.
- should recognise and attempt to compensate for the severe limitations of our ability to capture educational quality in performance indicators.
- provides well-founded and effective feedback that promotes insight into performance and supports good decision making about what should be celebrated and what should be changed.
- as a consequence of the [intelligent] accountability process, the majority of participants are more enthusiastic and motivated in their work (or at least not less enthusiastic and motivated).

I argue that the centrality of the superintendency in the educational system and the authority and influence vested in the position are not only key to promoting and supporting cultures of trust but are also key to developing and practice intelligent accountability, such as is outlined above. The superintendent's position in the education network and hierarchy affords multiple levels of influence including access to those who create policy, those who implement policy and those who work to support policy. This is especially so if superintendents consider themselves to be servant leaders.

SUMMARY

The office of the superintendency is as complex and multi-faceted as the concept of accountability is in public education contexts. While some connections between the two are clear and are defined in policy, others are hidden in the complexities of the relationships among various stakeholder groups. In this chapter I have established the centrality of the superintendency in facilitating various accountability relationships and in building strong trust cultures at all levels. By adopting and practicing intelligent accountability strategies and approaches, the office of the superintendency can contribute to the development of a larger system-wide understanding of education accountability that is based on trust and that supports trust cultures that can be renewed and sustained at local and provincial levels.

REFERENCES

Alberta Teachers' Association. (2006) *Accountability in education.* Edmonton, AB: Author.
Apple, M. W. (1993). *Official knowledge: Democratic education in a conservative age.* New York: Routledge.
Barlow, M., & Robertson, H. (1994). *Class warfare: The assault on Canada's schools.* Toronto: Key Porter Books.

Brown, P., Halsey, A. H., Lauder, H., & Wells, A. S. (1997). The transformation of education and society: An introduction. In A. H. Halsey, H. Lauder, P. Brown, & A. S. Wells (Eds.), *Education, culture, economy, and society* (pp. 1–44). Oxford: Oxford University Press.

Ben Jaafar, S., & Anderson, S. (2007). Policy trends and tensions in accountability for educational management and services in Canada. *Alberta Journal of Educational Research, 53*(2), 207–227.

Couture, J. C., & Liying, C. (2000). Teachers' work in the global culture of performance. *Alberta Journal of Educational Research, 46*(1), 65. Retrieved from the CBCA database.

Cowie, M., & Croxford, L. (2007). Intelligent accountability: Sound-bite or sea-change? *Centre for Educational Sociology (CES) Briefings, 43.* Retrieved February 17, 2009, from http://www.ces.ed.ac.uk/PDF%20Files/Brief043.pdf

Crippen, C. (2005) The democratic school: First to serve, then to lead. *Canadian Journal of Educational Administration and Policy, 47*, 1–17.

Crooks, T. (2003, April 22). *Some criteria for intelligent accountability applied to accountability in New Zealand.* Paper presented at the annual conference of the American Educational Research Association, Chicago, IL.

Dibski, D. (1979). Educational administration and policy making in the United States and Canada: Some observational differences. *Educational Studies, 10*(2), 163.

Elmore, R. F. (1979). Backward mapping: Implementation research and policy decisions. *Political Science Quarterly, 94*(4), 601–616.

Fleischman, J. (1990). A new framework for integration: Policy analysis and public management. *American Behavioral Scientist, 33*(6), 733.

Fullan, M. (2003). *The moral imperative of school leadership.* Thousand Oaks, CA: Corwin Press.

Fullan, M. (2004). *Leadership and sustainability: Systems thinkers in action.* Thousand Oaks, CA: Corwin Press.

Hopkins, D. (2005, June 24). *Accountability in the school system: An illustrative example from England* [PowerPoint slides]. Retrieved February 17, 2009, from www.oecd.org/dataoecd/63/62/35169510.ppt

Kaput, J., Bar-Yam, Y., Jacobson, M., Jakobsson, E., Lemke, J., & Wilensky, U. (2005). *Two roles for complex systems in education: Mainstream content and means for understanding the education system itself.* Retrieved March 13, 2009, from necsi.org/events/cxedk16/cxedk16_0.html

King, D. (2007, September). School principles: How should we shape our education system? A former minister weighs in. *Alberta Views, 10*, 32–35.

Krajewski, B., & Trevino, J. (2004). Building a culture of TRUST. *American School Board Journal, 191*(9), 32–34.

Kuchapski, R. (1998). Accountability and the social good: Utilizing Manzer's liberal framework in Canada. *Education and Urban Society, 30*(4), 531–545.

Leithwood, K., & Earl, L. (2000) Educational accountability effects: An international perspective. *Peabody Journal of Education, 75*(4), 1–18.

Levin, B. (2001). *Reforming education: From origins to outcomes.* London: RoutledgeFalmer.

Magolda, P. (2000). Being in the wrong place, wrong time: Re-thinking trust in qualitative inquiry. *Theory into Practice, 39*(3), 138–145.

Marginson, S. (1993). *Education and public policy in Australia.* Cambridge: Cambridge University Press.

Murgatroyd, S., & Henry, N. (2007). *Schools, accountability and performance: Critical issues document.* Edmonton, AB: Innovation Expedition.

O'Neill, O. (2002). *Called to account.* Retrieved March 13, 2009, from http://www.bbc.co.uk/radio4/reith2002/lecture3.shtml

Ranson, S. (2003). Public accountability in the age of neo-liberal governance. *Journal of Education Policy, 18*(5), 459–480.

Sahlberg P. (2007). Education policies for raising student learning: The Finnish approach. *Journal of Education Policy, 22*(2), 147–171.

School Act, R.S.A. c. S-3 (2000). Retrieved February 17, 2009, from http://www.qp.gov.ab.ca/documents/Acts/s03.cfm?frm_isbn=9780779733941

Shariff, S. (2006). Balancing competing rights: A stakeholder model for democratic schools. *Canadian Journal of Education, 29*(2), 476.

Taylor, A., Shultz, L., & Wishart Leard, D. (2005). A new regime of accountability for Alberta's public schools. In T. W. Harrison (Ed.), *The return of the Trojan horse: Alberta and the new world (dis)order* (pp. 236–253). Montreal: Black Rose Books.

Whitty, G., Power, S., & Halpin, D. (1998). *Devolution and choice in education: The school, the state and the market.* Buckingham, England: Open University Press.

DARREN KRASOWSKI

9. APPROACHES TO ACCOUNTABILITY

Possibilities for an Alternative Framework

Since the early 1990s, accountability has become a central feature in the educational systems of Western nations. What is evident through the implementation of various accountability models and programs, including those of my own province, Alberta, are tensions between what I refer to as the product-centred and process-centred approaches to educational accountability (Ben Jaafar & Anderson, 2007; Ranson, 2003). In this chapter, I outline the features of the two approaches and describe the tensions and contradictions that exist between them. I then argue that Alberta's current accountability framework relies too heavily on a product-centred approach, and I suggest a compromise between the product- and process-centred approaches. I base my proposal on the Finnish system of K-12 education, which holds public education accountable in the product-centred sense through the appropriate use of summative assessment data, and in the process-centred sense by giving voice to the professional judgement of teachers (Sahlberg, 2007; 2008a; 2008b).

PRODUCT-CENTRED ACCOUNTABILITY

To a great extent, the product-centred approach to educational accountability has been a response to the pressures of globalization that have increased over the past 20 years. Sahlberg (2008a) outlines five global trends that have influenced education: standardization, which focuses on outcomes-based education reforms; an increased focus on literacy and numeracy as the key controls in educational success; a search for safe and low-risk methods of teaching, thus reducing creative and divergent practices; a transfer of educational innovation, largely supported by world development organizations and encouraged by economic profit; and high-stakes accountability polices for evaluating schools and teachers. Ranson (2003) also refers to global trends, describing accountability as indicative of an age of neoliberalism. He identifies four types of neoliberal accountability: *consumer*, *contract*, *performative*, and *corporate*. He argues that education is strongly influenced by *performative* accountability: schools are accountable to the general public and answerable to government standards of education. In this product-centred approach, the purpose of accountability is to strengthen the quality of the "product" by evaluating school performance through the use of achievement targets and data that is derived from standardized tests. In this sense, polices that are in place are created to measure, judge and improve the performance of schools

K.D. Gariepy, B.L. Spencer and J.-C. Couture (eds.), Educational Accountability:
Professional Voices From the Field, 105–117.
© 2009 Sense Publishers. All rights reserved.

by rendering them continually accountable to external standards. As Poole (1993) argues:

> the best way to show [accountability] is through benchmarks, that is performance standards, and achievement levels which are reported publicly .... A first step toward accountability [is] regular formal assessment of student progress and publication of overall results in core subjects through standardized provincial systems. (as cited in Kuchapski, 1998, p. 531)

Ben Jaafar and Anderson (2007) describe this product-centred approach as *economic-bureaucratic accountability*, which "emphasizes a consumer-producer relationship ... where responsible individuals are accountable to an audience" (p. 211). In this description, responsibility for the improvement of public education rests on individual teachers and schools, who are accountable to hierarchal bodies for meeting set standards in student achievement. Here again, the focus is placed on results as the final product (i.e., output) of school systems.

Whether accountability is termed performative (Ranson, 2003) or economic-bureaucratic (Ben Jaafar & Anderson, 2007), the main assertion is that learning and education are quantifiable, measurable products and that schools are accountable for what they produce. In both of these product-centred approaches, the primary purpose of public education is to prepare students for participation in the global labour market.

PROCESS-CENTRED ACCOUNTABILITY

In the process-centred approach to educational accountability, learning is seen as a process, not a product. Ben Jaafar and Anderson (2007), Leithwood and Earl (2000) and Ranson (2003) argue for this approach to accountability because it emphasizes the role of professional judgement in determining the direction of school improvements. Ranson's (2003) explanation of educational accountability in the *age of professionalism* suggests that process-centred accountability can be informed by revisiting the conception of professional accountability that characterized public education in North America in the 1970s. This conception was based on a public trust in the ethical purposes of educators' work and the principles of teachers' professional practice, coupled with a commitment to a shared responsibility for student progress. In this sense, student progress and school improvement are accounted for in reports to local school authorities or boards and to parents and students. The account does not centre on "product" data gathered through standardized, summative assessments and is not subject to judgement of performance; rather, it centres on data compiled by qualified teachers through interim, formative assessments. Its purpose is to address the ongoing learning needs of students and to improve the quality of professional practice.

Leithwood and Earl's (2000) discussion of site-based management also presents a process-centred approach to accountability that "increases the power of teachers in school decision making while holding teachers more directly accountable for the school's effects on students" (p. 13). In this approach, teachers are collectively accountable to parents, students and central offices for the success of their school. Leithwood and Earl argue that the professionals closest to students possess the most relevant knowledge for determining directions and making decisions about school improvement. The responsibility for improvement and performance, then, shifts from being externally controlled to being internally controlled.

Ben Jaafar and Anderson (2007) describe this process-centred approach in terms of ethical-professional accountability (EPA), which moves away from a focus on a results-driven product and acknowledges the democratic purposes of education. While the product-centred approach focuses on preparing students to compete in the global marketplace, a process-centred, EPA approach focuses on preparing students to be citizens in a democratic society. Ben Jaafar and Anderson (2007) contend that educational accountability should place more importance on the means of schooling than on the ends. They see educational accountability as the shared, moral, professional responsibility of teachers, who, collectively and individually, are responsible for ongoing professional improvement. Blackmore (1988) supports this position, arguing that within the moral practice of the profession, teachers "should be accountable for the responsibilities one would normally associate with their position, and also for the actions they take or fail to take in process of meeting them" (p. 131).

Whether accountability reflects Ranson's (2003) call to earlier times when teachers where trusted to monitor student progress appropriately and to make improvements to their professional practice accordingly, Leithwood and Earl's (2000) idea of educator-involvement in site-based control over school decision making, or Ben Jaafar and Anderson's (2007) and Blackmore's (1998) view of teachers as accountable to the moral purposes of their profession, what is common to the all of these interpretations is a focus on process-centred accountability.

ALBERTA'S ACCOUNTABILITY FRAMEWORK

In Alberta, accountability constitutes one of three pillars (Funding, Flexibility and Accountability) of *Alberta Education's Renewed Funding Framework*. The *accountability pillar* "is based on a set of common factors that measure outcomes in specific categories, giving a clear picture of how well learning goals are being achieved" (Alberta Education, 2008). These specific categories are:
– safe and caring schools;
– student learning opportunities;
– student learning achievement (Grade K-9);
– student learning achievement (Grade 10 to 12);
– preparing for lifelong learning, employment and citizenship;
– parental involvement; and
– continuous improvement. (Alberta Education, 2006)

In this chapter, I draw on examples related mostly to the kindergarten to grade 9 (K-9) student learning achievement category, which includes data collected from Provincial Achievement Tests (PATs) that are written by all students in grades 3, 6, and 9. However, when referring to the *accountability pillar* and Alberta's accountability policies and framework, I am referring to all categories, which also include student learning achievement at the grade 10 to 12 level, comprising diploma exam results (standardized, exit exams in core subjects, usually taken by grade 12 students), numbers of provincial Rutherford Scholarships awarded to high school students and drop out and high school completion rates. I am also referring to the categories of safe and caring schools, student learning opportunities, preparing for lifelong learning, employment and citizenship, and parental involvement, all of which are evaluated through data collected from annual surveys of students, parents and teachers. The transition rate of students moving from high school into post-secondary education is also used to evaluate preparation for lifelong learning.

As part of the *Performance Management Cycle for School Authority Accountability*, the public reporting of achievement and survey results is an integral part of educational accountability (Alberta Education, 2007). Test results from the PATs are used to give an "achievement evaluation [that] is based on comparing the current school jurisdiction results for each measure (i.e. subject-specific standardized tests) against fixed standards... [which are based on a] three-year average... [and] yield an evaluation of Very High, High, Intermediate, Low, or Very Low" (Alberta Education, 2006). The evaluation of student learning achievement in the *Performance Management Cycle for School Authority Accountability*, then, is based on a "measurement"–student PAT scores. It is these test results that I refer to as the *product* in a product-centred accountability approach. The data resulting from these large-scale, standardized tests become a key indicator of the student learning achievement and education success and improvement at school, district and provincial levels.

TENSIONS BETWEEN THE ACCOUNTABILITY APPROACHES

Although, as Ben Jaafar and Anderson (2007) contend, "there is no single way to operationalize accountability in public education" (p. 209), based on the above description of the *accountability pillar*, I argue that Alberta's performance-driven accountability policies are operationalized through a product-centred approach to accountability. This, I suggest, is a problem not just because it puts emphasis on accountability of a certain type, for certain purposes, but also because it operates in a position of primacy over the many educational policies that regulate education in our province (Alberta Teachers' Association [ATA], 2005, 2006). While educators work towards the various aims and objectives that are outlined in other key policy documents such as Programs of Study (i.e., curriculum), to which they are also accountable, they are compelled to utilize the methods and strategies of a process-centred approach to accountability. However, the tensions involved in shifting between and working towards the often-competing purposes of the two approaches are frustrating and stressful to educators (Couture & Liying, 2000). Furthermore, within such challenging circumstances, the centrality of the product-centred approach to accountability may result in some unintended effects. In the following section I draw on literature that provides critiques of product-centred accountability approaches to develop an argument for re-thinking how accountability might operate in Alberta.

PROCESS- VERSUS PRODUCT-CENTRED LEARNING

Graves (2002) identifies seven qualities of the 21st century learner, none of which are testable. Qualities such as curiosity, sensitivity to others and initiative (p. 24) are difficult, if not impossible, to test on a paper-and-pencil exam. Murgatroyd (2008) suggests that the abilities to synthesize, be respectful of differences, and think ethically, creativity and "outside the box" are all necessary skills of the future. John Dewey believed that "the individual learning process [is] as unique as the human fingerprint" (Abbott, 2001, p. 87). What these thinkers agree on is that the individual act of learning, which can be described as the combination of processing information in order to grasp a concept, is not a product that can be measured against a set of predetermined standards. For example, of the twenty outcomes for basic education in Alberta, very few are products that can be assessed through product-based approaches to accountability (ATA, 2006). The emphasis on test and examination results inadequately represents the more inclusive, cultural, moral, creative and intellectual values related to lifelong learning and the democratic purposes of public education. Attributes and dispositions reflected in outcome descriptors such as *appreciate, respect, cooperate and empathize* that are found throughout the mandated Alberta curricula are assessed more appropriately by classroom teachers through process-centred accountability strategies.

FORMATIVE VERSUS SUMMATIVE ASSESSMENT

McEwen (2006) warns that "although most provincial assessments are designed to assess the achievement of provincial standards, many important learning outcomes cannot be measured by time-limited paper-and-pencil tests" (p 10). The degree to which all goals of education, teacher competency, student success and school quality can be judged by product-based accountability approaches is very limited. For example, summative assessments such as standardized tests that produce quantitative, comparative data give a general idea of how well an individual student has grasped learning objectives, but no more. Other process-based, formative types of monitoring are more appropriate for providing on-going assessments of student learning throughout a course of study. The tension occurs when teachers use a wide variety of strategies to assess student achievement throughout the year so as to be accountable for meeting the teaching and learning objectives of the Alberta curriculum but, in the end, the understandings and judgements related to educational accountability are tied so strongly to the *accountability pillar*.

In Alberta Education's (2006) *Renewed Funding Framework*, the phrase "holistic approach to evaluation" appears to be contradictory when the evidence upon which evaluation is based is limited to quantitative data consisting mostly of standardized test results and survey responses. Reporting data collected through a product-based accountability approach falls short of what most would understand to be a "holistic approach." Moreover, when such an approach is promoted as being holistic, there is a danger of the data being misinterpreted or misused, especially considering the obligation school districts have to publish their *accountability pillar* reports. There are a least two significant consequences of this.

First, poorly performing schools are scrutinized and an explanation for unsatisfactory results is expected. When the Ministry relies on the *accountability pillar* as the key arbitrator of school and system accountability, then increasing test scores becomes an all-encompassing task at the school and individual teacher level. The tension occurs when data gathered through standardized testing is used to pass judgment on student, teacher and school success. As Hargreaves (2009) argues, the danger of this is that internal pressure caused by externally mandated accountability policies can create schools that do not just react to targets, testing and published results, they "anticipate and prepare for them, scrutinizing and reorienting every program, curriculum choice, workshop, coaching session and teaching strategy in order to accommodate them" (p. 18). Through their research in Illinois, Stitzlein, Feinberg, Greene, & Miron, (2007) also found that experienced teachers described noticeable changes in their yearly plans as they hurried through potentially valuable lessons (for which objectives were not tested) and adjusted their teaching to ensure they covered testable objectives. The importance place on the standardized, one-size-fits-all approach to assessment can have the effect of pushing aside important educational objectives.

Second, when *accountability pillar* school-level data are used by media to report on the state of education and are picked up and published in rank order (e.g., by the Fraser Institute), individual schools and entire school districts are presented in a way that can identify them on a spectrum from "excellent and successful" to "poor and failing." As a result, all stakeholders in a school community experience the internal and external pressure to move up in the ranks, remain at the top, or avoid moving down. This takes the collection of product-based data beyond what is intended by the *accountability pillar* policy. Nevertheless, such publication of limited information indirectly passes judgement on quality of instruction and directly evaluates school performance. It turns the complexity of the educational process into a ranking of products, erodes public trust in education and undermines the many other ways in which accountability can be operationalized, shifting our sense of schools from communities of learners to audit cultures (Gewirtz, 2002).

TRUST VERSUS MISTRUST

Today, teachers exist in a product-centred context where accountability is based on a notion of trust that is linked to external assessment rather than internal, self-evaluation (Murgatroyd & Henry, 2007). What is implied in the use of widely-mandated, top down, product-centred accountability approaches is a mistrust of the general public in the professional teacher. Interestingly, McEwen (2006) found that this mistrust did not filter down to the parents of the students in community schools but remained in the perception of the general public. This could be a result of the overemphasis on product-centred accountability approaches or an effect of the way accountability data are often published, misinterpreted or misused. However, the tension remains because, as Ranson (2003) argues, the neoliberal accountability policies that were designed and intended to restore trust to public services have had the unforeseen result of further eroding public trust

because [they have] embodied flawed criteria of evaluation and relations of accountability ... [where] the dominant mode of answerability cannot deliver achievement because it defines a mistaken criteria of evaluating performance, [through] emphasizing the external imposition of targets and quantifiable outcomes ... at the expense of a pedagogy that works 'inside-out'. (p. 470)

The above critiques and explanations of the effects of the competing conceptions of product- and process-based accountability approaches may be helpful in understanding some of the accountability tensions that currently exist in Alberta. To move from a focus on process rather than product, formative instead of summative assessment and a context of trust instead of mistrust, I suggest that Alberta consider the accountability framework of the Finnish system of public education.

KEY POLICIES OF THE FINNISH APPROACH TO EDUCATIONAL ACCOUNTABILITY

Finland has etched a path in education on which accountability is understood in terms of both a strong economy and a strong democracy. The Finnish system has produced a

multi-cultural, high-tech knowledge economy accepting an active role in shaping the present-day European economic ... environment ... [and has an] educational system [that] has become an attractive and internationally examined example of a well-performing system that successfully combines quality with wide-spread equity and social cohesion through reasonable public financing. (Sahlberg, 2007 p. 147)

In the early 1990s, Finland adopted an accountability approach that is highly process-centred. Sahlberg illustrates the success of Finnish education on the global stage, pointing to high participation rates, low variance in student performance across schools (i.e., low degree of social inequality), and Programme for International Student Assessment (PISA) scores in reading, mathematics and science that are among the best of all OECD participants, including Alberta. To explain Finland's success, Sahlberg identifies three key polices priorities: loose and flexible standards, objectives for broad learning and creativity, and intelligent accountability. Those of us who wonder about the effectiveness of Alberta's present product-centred approach to educational accountability can potentially learn from the policy directions of the Finnish system.

LOOSE AND FLEXIBLE STANDARDS AND INTERNAL CONTROL OF EDUCATION

In Finland, a general national framework for curriculum and standards allows plenty of room for innovative practices and experimentation. Professional freedom and public trust are granted to teachers so that curriculum and programs can be developed to focus on student learning. Teacher and school autonomy result in the ability of schools to optimize resources and to individualize instructional time to best meet the needs of students (Sahlberg, 2007). Furthermore, Sahlberg (2008b) explains that flexibility also exists in the reporting of student progress and achievement and is "promoted by freedom of choice, decentralized management, and a culture of trust in professional communities" (p. 10). Such flexibility and internal control, Sahlberg (2007) suggests, is "rare ... in more rigid and test-heavy systems" (p. 156).

BROAD, CREATIVE LEARNING

A guiding principle in the Finnish model is the creation of broad learning objectives with the encouragement from policymakers to continually strive for excellence in learning. Finland places learning first and a prudent sampling of curriculum knowledge second. It does so because of a society that recognizes the importance of learning over testing. This approach to education is supported at all levels. For example, large corporations, such as Nokia, have reminded education policymakers of the value of creativity and innovation in teaching and learning and have discouraged a standardized system dependent upon national testing. As Sahlberg (2008b) argues, when learning is the primary goal and there is no need to focus on annual tests, teachers are encouraged to take risks in their teaching, to be innovative in their practices, and try new, creative teaching methods as a long as these initiatives are regarded by the profession as appropriate for improving student learning. The only standardized, high-stakes test taken by Finnish students is at the end of upper secondary school (grade 12). Additional external government tests are used with a random sampling, but with this exception, Finnish schools are external test-free zones.

INTELLIGENT ACCOUNTABILITY AND PROFESSIONAL TRUST

Intelligent accountability in Finland involves all stakeholders in determining whether or not collectively established goals have been achieved. Sahlberg (2008b) explains that this mutual planning draws on data from student self-assessments, teacher-led classroom assessments, school internal evaluations and external examinations. He contends that this approach to accountability draws upon samples rather than census. Education in Finland has been built upon sustained leadership, values rooted in equality and equitable distribution of resources, and trust among education stakeholders, specifically teachers. Finland has set high standards for teachers and teaching is viewed by Finnish society as a high-status profession. For example, when governments regarded teachers as competent professionals by involving them in curriculum reform, what resulted was a mutual, motivated and engaged effort to improve the education system. Teachers actively develop their own knowledge and skills through a program of continued professional development where "continuous upgrading of teachers' pedagogical professionalism has become a right rather than an obligation" (Sahlberg, 2007, p.

155). Such intelligent accountability has preserved and enhanced trust in teachers and has encouraged a strong sense of responsibility and initiative in the professional (Sahlberg, 2007). Sahlberg (2008b) argues that "fear-free" schools create innovative practices, creative learning environments and strong professional learning cultures.

USING THE FINNISH MODEL TO MODIFY
ALBERTA'S EDUCATIONAL ACCOUNTABILITY

Product- and Process-centred Education

I argue that, currently, Alberta's *accountability pillar*, with the data collected and reported as mandated by the province's accountability policy framework, has taken on a life of its own. The tension exists in our context because the importance of testing curriculum content seems to be the prime objective, superseding learning. In the Finnish model, learning comes first and the measuring of knowledge comes second (Sahlberg, 2007). The establishment of a general, national set of standards in the Finnish curriculum resonates with a product-centred approach to accountability, but by having flexibility within these standards so that learning and instruction can be individualized, a process-centred approach is central. If, in Alberta, we aspire to develop innovative thinkers within a knowledge-based society, then we must acknowledge that both process- and product-centred approaches must co-exist and be represented in and supported by the government-mandated accountability framework.

Formative and Summative Assessments by Professional Educators

As is the case in Finland, creating general curriculum objectives and standards that can be interpreted and implemented by the professional educator is critical to a healthy accountability system. Such an approach could be encouraged in Alberta so that schools might better meet the needs of individual learners and respond to their unique and complex communities. Sahlberg (2008b) acknowledges the need for an accountability system where a balance between qualitative and quantitative measures co-exists in "mutual accountability, professional responsibility, and trust" (p.15). Within a framework that places importance on both product- and process-centred approaches to accountability, the role of the government would be to ensure that curricula are being covered through prudent, random sampling in a modified testing program that would provide benchmark data at the provincial, district and school levels. Students would not pass or fail these tests, but the data would be provided to district and school administrators who, in turn, would share the results with teaching staff and the parent community. Just as the expert role of a physician is to decipher the results of a CAT scan, it would be the role of the professional educator to read and assess test data and to extract what is important for improving teaching practice. In this way, large-scale achievement test data would not form the basis of statistical punishment for poorly performing schools, but instead would open up a professional conversation for possible program changes.

In the compromise of the two approaches to educational accountability, the role of assessment is integral. If one is to accept the importance of the process-centred approach, then formative assessments and alternative measurements that acknowledge individual learning must play a more important role in policy frameworks, such as that of the *accountability pillar*. Here, Ranson's (2003) ideas about professional accountability reflect some significant principles: What is being accounted for is student progress, not standards, and the purpose is to meet the needs of student learning not to produce a better quality product. As Ben Jaafar and Anderson (2007) state, EPA, which reflects a process-centred approach, shifts the emphasis from being accountable to an external party to being accountable for a process "where the means are emphasized over the ends" (p. 211). Continuous and ongoing learning should be measured and assessed by the classroom teacher, who has intimate knowledge of the capabilities and context of the individual student. A process-centred approach based on professional judgment correctly assumes the assessment of learning can take into consideration many forms of measurement and assessment, and resists the tendency to place inordinate importance on numerical data as the indicator of growth. The control of improving educational achievement shifts from an external party to an internal one as teachers, schools and educational specialists share a common responsibility based on the ethical, moral purpose of their work, which is supported by the trust of external agencies such as elected officials and government bodies. This professional control increases the influence of teachers in school decision-making and holds teachers, collectively, accountable to parents, students, and central offices for the performance of their school (Leithwood & Earl, 2000).

Public Accountability through High Standards, Shared Responsibility and Mutual Trust

In a system where product- and process-centred accountability approaches are valued for their appropriate uses, questions about *to whom* teachers are accountable are answered and teacher professionalism is also valued. Leithwood and Earl (2000) support the use of standards to hold individual teachers accountable to the public for the delivery of instruction but further suggest the following guidelines related to licensure:

> The professional is held accountable to the government and, beyond the license, to one's professional association of colleagues. Standards require professionals to justify failure to practice in ways consistent with the standards…[and such] failure to comply with standards carries the potential of being barred from entry to the profession, being censured, being limited in one's professional activities, and being removed from the profession. (p. 14)

This proposal suggests that high standards for the profession are turned over to members of the profession, such as through professional associations like the Alberta Teachers' Association.

Hargreaves (2009) suggests that creating highly qualified teachers is not about quick fixes or higher qualifications, but about the purpose, esteemed status, working conditions, the rewards of the job as well as timely training. The establishment of sound practices through effective teacher mentorship programs are essential in maintaining high standards. Hargreaves argues that these collaborative approaches not only have an impact on student success but improve the retention of new teachers. In light of these points, I argue that in Alberta, once in the profession, new teachers should work collaboratively with an experienced mentor(s) for the first year and, after that, as is the case in Finland, continuous professional learning should be an expectation and a right of being a teacher.

Shared Responsibility

An accountability framework that acknowledges both product- and process-centred approaches to accountability must emphasize, as the Finnish system does, that education is the responsibility of all stakeholders. As Linn (2003) summarizes, this "true accountability means a broadly shared responsibility, not only among educators and students, but also administrators, policy-makers, parents, and educational researchers. That is, accountability means we all share responsibility for improving education" (p. 10). In this view, assessment information about students and schools is distributed to whom the account is owed. Such an approach prevents the unfair evaluation of schools based on the performance of standardized tests alone and encourages a collective responsibility and a mutual understanding of the complexity of education and learning.

Where an inherent trust exists between all partners and each is responsible to play their role in improving teaching and learning, accountability in Alberta would be something done with schools, not to them. As Sahlberg (2008b) suggests, "first, build trust and collective responsibility in schools and their communities" (p. 21). In a new accountability system, trust would become the foundation for the establishment of all other policies. This is achieved through the acknowledgement of the key role that professional teachers play in the judgment of performance in education and the evaluation and measurement of growth in learning. Sahlberg (2007) contends that "the culture of trust simply means that education authorities and political leaders believe that teachers, together with principals, parents and their communities, know how to provide the best possible education for their children and youth" (p. 157).

When public funds are used to support and operate an educational system, it can be assumed, from the product-centred perspective, that education is a product. To test the effectiveness of any product the collection of data is helpful in determining the quality of performance. Large-scale, standardized tests and surveys are appropriate ways of collecting such data. However, as Ranson (2003) argues, the idea of professionals being inspected and watched over by a public that is dependent upon honest media opinion is archaic and calls for the "public to restore control of public services to the professional specialist, whose accountability resides in the presentation of information" (p. 471). He further suggests that giving voice to the public sector promotes an environment of trust and mutual accountability. I suggest that the Finnish system of intelligent accountability (Sahlberg, 2008b) could be adopted in Alberta. In this way, teachers would be accountable for educational outcomes and directions that are mutually agreed upon in the school community; however, because this process is two directional, the community stakeholders (such as school boards and departments of education) would be accountable for ensuring that schools have all the necessary resources, conditions and opportunities to achieve the agreed upon goals.

CONCLUDING THOUGHTS

In this chapter, I have defined product-centred and process-centred approaches to accountability and I have discussed how these approaches are operationalized in the Alberta context in ways that result in tensions in our public school system. I have outlined some key principles of Finland's accountability model to suggest a compromise for Alberta's accountability framework. If we are at all interested in redefining accountability in Alberta, we will need to find a path where there is a harmony between the expectations of the market economy and the social democratic values of learning. In the accountability framework that I recommend, there would be assessments for collecting data on the product of education as well as on the process of learning. Stakeholders would need to come together as a community to create new accountability roles that are based on mutual respect, trust and responsibility. Accountability, then, would define and promote an educational system that is innovative, flexible and effective–one that leaves the ambiguous questions of test-driven accountability behind and establishes a responsible group of dedicated parties with a common vision, where "accountability, is really responsibility to each other" (Hargreaves, 2008).

REFERENCES

Abbott, J., & Ryan, T. (2001). *The unfinished revolution: Learning, human behavior, community, and political paradox*. Alexandria, VA: Association for Supervision and Curriculum Development.

Alberta Education. (2006). Renewed framework for funding school jurisdictions. In Alberta Education, *2006-2007 funding manual for school authorities*. Retrieved February 2, 2009, from http://education.alberta.ca/media/482898/framework.pdf

Alberta Education. (2007). *Guide for education planning and results reporting: Requirements for Alberta school jurisdictions (public, separate and Francophone school authorities) and their schools*. Retrieved February 2, 2009, from http://education.alberta.ca/media/441524/SchoolBoardGuideFinalMar06-07.pdf

Alberta Education. (2008). *About the accountability pillar*. Retrieved February 2, 2009, from http://education.alberta.ca/admin/funding/accountability/about.aspx

Alberta Teachers' Association. (2005). *Accountability in education*. Edmonton, AB: Author.

Alberta Teachers' Association. (2006). *Handle with care: Futures being built*. Paper presented at the Invitational Symposium on Educational Accountability, Edmonton, AB.

Ben Jaafar, S., & Anderson, S. (2007). Policy trends and tensions in accountability for educational management and services in Canada. *Alberta Journal of Educational Research, 53*(2), 207–227.

Blackmore, J. (1988). *Assessment and accountability*. Geelong, Australia: Deakin University Press.

Couture, J. C., & Liying, C. (2000). Teachers' work in the global culture of performance. *Alberta Journal of Educational Research, 46*(1), 65.

Gewirtz, S. (2002). *The managerial school: Post-welfarism and social justice in education.* New York: Routledge.

Graves, D. H. (2002). *Testing is not teaching: What should count in education.* Portsmouth, NH: Heinemann.

Hargreaves, A. (2008, April 18). *Sustaining teacher leadership: Necessary conditions for a culture of innovation.* Paper presented at the Symposium on Leadership in Educational Accountability: Sustaining Professional Learning and Innovation in Alberta Schools, Edmonton, AB.

Hargreaves, A. (2009). The fourth way of change: Towards an age of inspiration and sustainability. In A. Hargreaves & M. Fullan (Eds.), *Change wars.* Bloomington, IN: Solution Tree.

Kuchapski, R. (1998). Accountability and the social good: Utilizing Manzer's liberal framework in Canada. *Education and Urban Society, 30*(4), 531–545.

Leithwood, K., & Earl, L. (2000). Educational accountability effects: An international perspective. *Peabody Journal of Education, 75*(4), 1–18.

Linn, R. L. (2003). Accountability: Responsibility and reasonable expectations. *Educational Researcher, 32*(7), 3–13.

McEwen, N. (2006). *The impact of educational accountability in Alberta since 1995.* Paper presented at the Canadian Society for the Study of Education Annual Conference, Toronto, ON.

Murgatroyd, S. (2008, April 18). *Focusing accountability on the learner.* Paper presented at the Symposium on Leadership in Educational Accountability: Sustaining Professional Learning and Innovation in Alberta Schools, Edmonton, AB.

Murgatroyd, S., & Henry, N. (2007). *Schools, accountability and performance: Critical issues document.* Edmonton, AB: Innovation Expedition.

Ranson, S. (2003). Public accountability in the age of neo-liberal governance. *Journal of Education Policy 18*(5), 459–480.

Sahlberg P. (2007). Education policies for raising student learning: The Finnish approach. *Journal of Education Policy, 22*(2), 147–171.

Sahlberg, P. (2008a). *From periphery to limelight: Educational change in Finland.* Unpublished manuscript.

Sahlberg, P. (2008b, April 18). *Real learning first: Accountability in a knowledge society.* Paper presented at the Symposium on Leadership in Educational Accountability: Sustaining Professional Learning and Innovation in Alberta Schools, Edmonton, AB.

Stitzlein, S. M., Feinberg, W., Greene, J., & Miron, L. (2007). Illinois project for democratic accountability. *Educational Studies: Journal of the American Educational Studies Association, 42*(2), 139–155.

ABOUT THE CONTRIBUTORS

Jean-Claude (J-C) Couture is Executive Assistant (Government) of the Alberta Teachers' Association (ATA). Before joining the Association in 1999, he taught high school social studies in Hinton, Alberta for 20 years. Throughout his career, J-C has been an active member of the teaching profession, serving as a sublocal president, chair of his local's political involvement committee and as a member of his local's economic policy committee. Later, he advanced teachers' interests at the provincial level by serving as a member of the ATA's Curriculum Committee and as an ATA representative to Alberta Education's Senior High Program Coordinating Committee.

Alanna Crawford lives in Barrhead, Alberta, where she has taught senior high mathematics at the Alberta Distance Learning Centre for 7 years. She has also taught in the Alberta towns of Desmarais, Irma and Mayerthorpe. Alanna is currently pursuing her MEd in the Department of Educational Policy Studies at the University of Alberta, and in her spare time, she and her husband, Stephen, enjoy camping, hiking, backpacking and cross country skiing in the Canadian Rockies.

Troy Davies holds a BA in political science from the University of Regina, a BEd in secondary education from McGill University and an MEd in educational leadership from the University of Calgary. He is currently a PhD student in the Department of Educational Policy Studies at the University of Alberta. For the past nine years, he has been both a vice principal and principal. Troy's research interests are school leadership, the marketization of education, school choice and complexity/chaos theories. He lives in Edmonton with his wife and three sons.

Kelli Ewasiuk is currently working on her MEd in the Department of Educational Policy Studies at the University of Alberta. She is interested in current trends in early literacy development and literacy as it relates to equity in education. She has been an elementary school teacher and a reading intervention specialist. She lives in Edmonton with her two children, Stephanie and Ashley, where she is a literacy coordinator with the Edmonton Catholic School District.

Kenneth D. Gariepy is a critical librarian and a PhD student in the Department of Educational Policy Studies at the University of Alberta. He also teaches in the Faculty of Business at Athabasca University and in the School of Library and Information Studies at the University of Alberta. His areas of research interest include intellectual freedom policy and social justice issues in public and school libraries.

Patricia Gervais holds an MES from the University of Alberta and combined Bachelor of Music/Bachelor of Education degrees from the University of Lethbridge. She was an elementary school teacher for eighteen years, during which time she taught French immersion, music, language arts, remedial reading and early intervention. Patricia is also an experienced school administrator and special education coordinator. Currently, she is the special education coordinator for St. Paul Education Regional Division No. 1. She and her husband have four children.

Randy Hetherington is the principal of a high school in rural Alberta and has been a classroom teacher, department head, PD trainer and school administrator. He is also a PhD student in the Department of Educational Policy Studies at the University of Alberta and is interested in the role of the superintendent as an agent of change. He lives in the County of Lac Ste. Anne with his wife, Michele, and their daughter, Kyra, with whom he shares a passion for learning.

Heather Kennedy-Plant is a passionate community and family advocate. She has worked at the University of Alberta since 1999 and is currently a cooperative education coordinator in the School of Business. Heather has a BA in sociology from the University of Alberta and is working towards her MEd in educational policy studies.

Darren Krasowski has been an elementary school teacher and administrator for over 20 years, during which time he has gained personal insights into the effects of educational accountability on the classroom. He is working on his MEd at the University of Alberta and lives in Edmonton with his wife, Dana, and sons, Logan and Gavin.

Pasi Sahlberg is an educator and school improvement activist. He has experience in educational reforms, training teachers and leaders, coaching schools to change and advising education policy-makers around the world. His main areas of interest are educational change, school improvement and global education policies. His working record includes teaching, teacher training, research, state-level administration (Ministry of Education in Finland) and international education development (World Bank, OECD, European Union). He has a PhD from the University of Jyväskylä (Finland) and is an adjunct professor at the University of Helsinki and the University of Oulu.

Brenda L. Spencer is an assistant professor in the Department of Educational Policy Studies at the University of Alberta. Her academic interests include the sociology and politics of education and reform, policy and practice, equity studies, urban schools and educational leadership. Her work draws on critical theories of power and the state, globalization and social geography. Brenda's current research examines how policies for accountability organize and construct the knowledges, practices, conditions and spaces of public education.

Shelley Willier is a First Nations educator who has held leadership positions in provincial and federal education authorities. Currently, she is principal of Atikameg School for Whitefish Lake First Nation #459 and is completing her MEd in Indigenous Peoples education at the University of Alberta. Her graduate work focuses on First Nations identity, leadership models and accountability structures.

INDEX

Printed in the United States
145264LV00003B/2/P